Respectfully Yours, Wm. T. King.

History of the
American Steam
Fire-Engine

William T. King

DOVER PUBLICATIONS, INC.
Mineola, New York

Published in Canada by General Publishing Company, Ltd., 30 Lesmill Road, Don Mills, Toronto, Ontario.

Bibliographical Note

This Dover edition, first published in 2001, is an unabridged republication of the work originally published by the author in 1896.

Library of Congress Cataloging-in-Publication Data

King, William T.
    History of the American steam fire-engine / William T. King.
        p. cm.
    Originally published: Boston : Pinkham Press, 1896.
    ISBN 0-486-41530-9 (pbk.)
     1. Fire engines. 2. Steam-engines. I. Title.

TH9376 .K5 2001
629.225—dc21

00-065811

Manufactured in the United States of America
Dover Publications, Inc., 31 East 2nd Street, Mineola, N.Y. 11501

CONTENTS.

iv CONTENTS.

LIST OF ILLUSTRATIONS.

PREFACE.

So little honor was done the man who first forged harness for the giant, Steam, that even the time of his death is unknown and his last resting-place remains unnoticed.

For nearly two thousand years, the potential power of water in the form of steam was known to mankind. Generations of scholars and scientists found the subject of steam an amusing theme for learned speculation or for pleasing experiments. Philosophers settled down to the belief that steam could not be applied to commercial purposes. Theoretical investigators had given up steam as beyond their control, when Thomas Newcomer, working blacksmith, directed his attention to it. This was in the beginning of the eighteenth century, when mechanical skill was at a low ebb.

The first engine was a piston, working in a cylinder and transmitting power to a walking beam. Although it was exceedingly crude, it possessed the essential principle of all succeeding steam-engines, the cylinder and piston.

Before any radical improvement was made on the engine, they were built and used successfully for pumping purposes all over Europe, many of them coming to America. Newcomer was really the father of mechanical engineering; yet the Royal Society for the Promotion of Science did not think his work was worthy of notice, and his disciples, who are now legion, cannot point to the spot where his dust reposes. Unfortunately, he lived in a time when it had not become the fashion to honor the heroes of industry.

A great many steam fire-engines have been built which proved a failure, which might have proved good, practical machines, had they not fallen into the hands of men who were prejudiced against that particular build, or through a lack of knowledge how to run and care for them. The man in charge should be a practical engineer; not, necessarily, a machinist, but a man who is quick to think and act. He should have a thorough knowledge of steam and steam machinery; should be capable, also, of adjusting all the different parts of his engine, and telling whether they are in order or not. He should fully understand the causes of deterioration in the boilers of this kind of machines and the best means of protecting them from the evils which endanger their safety and limit their usefulness. He should have, if not a thorough, a tolerably good knowledge of hydraulics and hydraulic machines and be capable of determining their capacity, and understanding the strains to which they are subjected when in use.

These qualifications, to a great extent, have been heretofore overlooked, and the reader, if a fireman, needs not to be told the reasons why.

That the duties which this class of men is expected to perform are of a very important character, all will admit; and it would be difficult to assign any reasonable cause why they should not be encouraged to qualify themselves for their faithful and intelligent performance.   And while it is a fact that many of the men in charge of steam fire-engines are capable and intelligent engineers, yet, unfortunately, they are not all so ; nor will they ever be so as a body until they receive their appointments on real merit instead of through political influence, and are retained in the service during good behavior and encouraged to improve themselves.

But the days of steam fire-engines are numbered.   As the steamer took the place of the hand-engine, so will the water works take the place of the steamer; for the Holly system of direct pressure, or a high gravity, is much more desirable.   We are living in an age of progression ; and there is hardly a great thing invented before something far superior takes its place.   So, when the days of the steam fire-engine are no more, we can look back with pride and say, " Farewell, you good and faithful servants."

THE STEAM FIRE-ENGINE.

" Behold!   How she shines in her beauty,
    Resplendent in silver and gold;
Ne'er shrinking from doing her duty,
    When worked by her members so bold;
So peacefully-innocent standing,
    You'd dream not the work she can do;
But when we her aid are demanding,
    She always proves faithful and true.

" We look on her with admiration,
    Well knowing the work she can do;
She's full of life and animation;
    Her duty she seems to know, too;—
She saves us a deal of hard labor,
    Her muscles seem never to tire—
Admired by stranger and neighbor,
    Whene'er she's at work at a fire.

" Oh! dear shall she be to us ever;—
    For she's our companion and friend;
She does her work neatly and clever,
    And labors, with zeal, to the end;
The Steamer!   We'll ever adore you;
    In praising you we never tire;
Hand-engines were nothing before you,
    Nor compared with you when at a fire."

(*Fireman's Herald*, March 9, 1882.)

History of the American Steam Fire-Engine.

GEORGE BRAITHWAITE — LONDON, 1829.

This history is supposed to speak only of American steam fire-engines; but it is only just and proper that a short account should be given of the first steam fire-engine

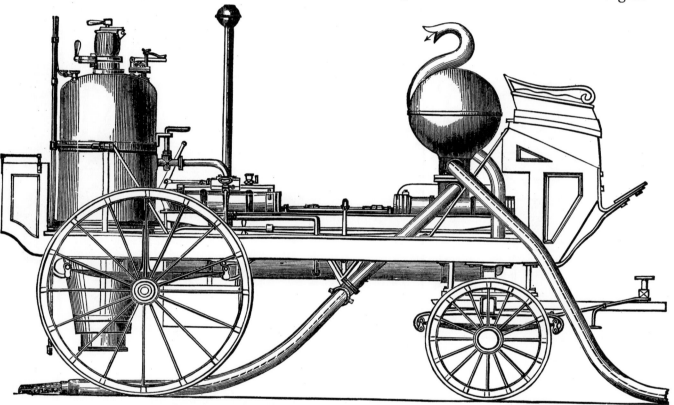

FIRST STEAM FIRE-ENGINE EVER BUILT—LONDON, 1829.
The "Novelty," George Braithwaite, Builder.

ever built in the world, in order to give the reader a better idea of the great progress made in this useful piece of machinery.

To England belongs the credit of conceiving the idea, and to America belongs the honor of perfecting the invention; and, as a result, the American steam fire-engine of to-day, in symmetry of parts, elegance of finish and efficiency of action stands unrivalled by any other in the world.

In the year 1829, the first steam fire-engine ever built was made in London by George Braithwaite, a celebrated hydraulic engineer, assisted by Capt. John Ericsson, the great inventor, who was afterwards made famous in this country by designing the ironclad *Monitor.*

This first steam fire-engine was named "Novelty"; weight, 2¼ tons; and rated as ten horse power. The pumps measured 6½ inches in diameter and steam cylinders, 7½ inches

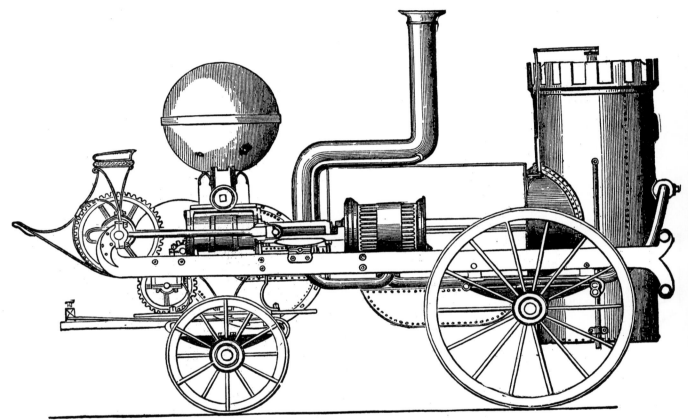

BRAITHWAITE'S FOURTH ENGINE—THE "COMET."
Built for the King of Prussia, in 1832.

in diameter, were double and placed horizontally; each steam piston, and that of the pump, being attached to one rod. The waste steam from the cylinders was sent through the feed water tank by means of two coiled pipes; thus warming the feed water before it was pumped into the boiler, which was vertical, with fire-box tapering downward. The fuel was burned on the forced combustion principle; that is to say, it was fed into the boiler from the top, and was burned in a closed fire-box, the products of combustion passing from the furnace to the chimney by means of a long snake-like tube which extended below the water line several times from end to end of the long barrel of the boiler, and finally passed out at the forward end, near to and above the air-chamber of the pump.

This machine would throw 200 to 250 gallons of water per minute to the height of 90 feet. It was run to a number of fires in London and abundantly illustrated its great value; but every effort of its builders to secure its adoption in the fire service of the metropolis proved in vain, as both the public and the fire insurance companies were bitterly opposed to its use. Despite the refusal of the English to take hold of the novel fire extinguishing apparatus, Braithwaite and his partner succeeded in convincing less prejudiced communities of the utility of their machine and built several more.

The one that attracted the most notice was that built for the king of Prussia, in 1832, to protect the public buildings in Berlin. This was his fourth engine and it was named " Comet." The boiler was on the same plan as that of the " Novelty," with few exceptions. It had double cylinders and pumps working horizontally; steam cylinder 12x14, pumps 10½x14, and would run from 18 to 25 strokes per minute, through from one to four lines of hose. Steam could be got up to a pressure of 70 lbs. in 20 minutes, and through a 1¼ in. nozzle, a stream was ejected to the height of 115 ft. It consumed three bushels of coke per hour. Its cost was £1,200 or $6,000.

The success of this engine brought Braithwaite much complimentary notice in Prussia, but the Londoners would have none of the new-fangled machines and stuck to their hand-tubs, of which they use a great many at the present day.

His fifth and last engine was built in 1833, and was only an experiment. The boiler was of locomotive pattern. All of his engines were horizontal, without fly-wheels, and with straight frame.

Discouraged and disheartened he gave up his invention, and seven years afterward Americans took the matter in hand, and, although it was an up-hill fight, at last succeeded in convincing the world that steam was far superior to muscle.

P. R. HODGE—1840.

The first Steam Fire-Engine ever built in the United States was built by Paul Rapsey Hodge, an eminent English engineer, in New York City, in 1840–41.

The alarming frequency and extent of fires in the city of New York during the winter of 1839–40 caused the attention of the citizens generally, and of the insurance companies in particular, to be directed to the subject of providing more efficient means for extinguishing fires than then existed. At the suggestion of the underwriters, Paul Rapsey Hodge, an ingenious mechanical engineer of Laight St., was commissioned by the insurance companies to build a Steam Fire-Engine ; the conditions being that the engine

HODGE'S STEAM FIRE ENGINE.

should be drawn by either men or horses, and should throw a stream of water over the flag-staff of the City Hall.

The work was commenced December 12, 1840, and completed in the spring of 1841. The engine very much resembled a locomotive, and was very heavy. It was publicly tested in front of the City Hall on Saturday afternoon, March 27, 1841, at 4 P. M. It threw a 1½ in. stream over the flag-staff, and was approved by the authorities.

It was now that the trouble commenced. The firemen of New York were jealous of the new comer. They wrought themselves up to a bitter opposition ; for, if allowed to work, it would distance all competitors and render hand-engines of no account, and the occupation of " Mose " and " The B'hoys " would be gone. The great trouble now was to get a company to work her ; and for some time she lay an elephant on the insurance company's hands. The firemen shrank from it; it was novel; it foreboded change. Its owners finally applied to the foreman of the Pearl Hose Co., No. 28, to take charge of it. He submitted the matter to his company, who, upon motion of George W. Lane, unanimously determined to man her, and to the Pearl Hose Co., No. 28, belongs the honor of using the first Steam Fire-Engine in America.

After a few months' use, it was given up. It is but justice to say that the employment of steam fire-engines was at that time very unpopular; and the firemen found fault with the working of the engine, claiming that she was too heavy and that the boiler would not furnish steam enough, etc. These probably were faults which could easily have been remedied and improvements made in building another. But the insurance companies became satisfied that with hostility on the part of the firemen, their losses would be increased rather than diminished; and the steamer was withdrawn and sold to a Mr. Bloomer, a packing-box manufacturer, who used it for a stationary engine.

Hodge's engine, which looked like a locomotive, was 13½ feet long, and weighed between 7 and 8 tons. The engine was self propelling. The rear running-wheels were made of wrought iron and were used as balance wheels when working at a fire. As soon as the engine was located where it was to get the supply of water, the rear end of the engine would be raised clear of the ground by means of a jack-screw and the wheels used as balance-wheels. The main axle was divided by a sleeve socket joint; but when jacked up and in working order, a clutch-pin connected the axle and brought the two crank-pins on the wheel faces at right angles to each other. The connecting rods were then attached. The steam cylinders were 9½ in. by 14 in. The pumps were 8¼ in. by 14 in. The pumps and steam cylinders lay horizontally, one on either side; and were attached to the smoke-box of the boiler. The pumps had receiving-screws on either side, and delivery-screws on the front end. The boiler was of the locomotive style (Bury style), tubular, with flaring fire-box and steam dome. The piston-rods worked through engine and pump direct. Once, on a trial, she threw a stream to the height of 166 ft., making 120 revolutions per minute.

JOHN ERICSSON—1841.

The name of Capt. John Ericsson is well known to all; and, although he never built an American Steam Fire-Engine, I purpose to make mention of him as it has been reported that he did, and several suppose it to be so; for that reason, I will furnish the reader with the facts.

This noted man and great inventor was born in the Province of Wermland, Sweden, in 1803, and came to this country in 1839. In the year 1840, the Mechanics' Institute,

ERICSSON'S DESIGN FOR ENGINE.

in New York City, offered a gold medal for the best design for a steam fire-engine, and Ericsson received the prize. The publication of the notice was very limited, and but two or three plans were sent in. The Committee, after a careful examination of the several plans and specifications offered, reported in favor of the one presented by Ericsson. In the report was the following paragraph: " The points of excellence, as thus narrowed down, were found to belong, in a superior degree, to an engine weighing less than two

(6)

and a half tons, that, with the lowest estimate of speed, has a power of 108 men, and will throw 3,000 lbs. of water per minute to a height of 105 ft., through a 1½ in. nozzle. By increasing the speed to the greatest limit easily and safely attainable, the quantity of water thrown may be much augmented."

In this design, the force-pump was double acting, and placed directly under the air-chamber; the latter being globular in form. Between the two were the delivery pipes, one on either side, and below the pump, the suction pipe. The boiler, which was horizontal, was of the locomotive style, and was to contain 27 tubes, 1½ in. in diameter. Forward of all was a blowing apparatus, consisting of a square wooden box with parallel sides, in which a piston worked, attached to the sides by leather. The air was to be forced by this piston into a reservoir above, provided with a movable top, from whence it was to be conveyed to the furnace. The inventor calculated that he could get up a working head of steam in ten minutes.

This engine was never built, and the general belief that Ericsson constructed an engine in this country is erroneous. In order to give the reader a better idea of the plans and working of this engine, I will describe the drawings. Had this engine been built according to plans laid out, it would undoubtedly have proved a very practical machine, and been the cause of bringing the steam fire-engine to perfection long before it was.

DESCRIPTION OF THE DRAWINGS.

Figure 1—Side view of the steam fire-engine complete.

Figure 2—Represents the longitudinal section of the boiler, steam engine, pump, air-vessel and blowing apparatus, through the centre line.

Figure 3—Plan or top view of the engine; air-vessel, slide box of steam-cylinder and induction pipe supposed to be removed.

Figure 4—Transverse section of the boiler, through the furnace and steam-chamber.

Figure 5—Lever or handle for working the blowing apparatus by manual labor.

Similar letters of reference will be used to denote similar parts in all of the figures.

A—Double acting force-pump, cast of gun metal, firmly secured to the carriage frame by four strong brackets cast. *a, a,* Suction valves. *a¹, a¹,* Suction passages leading to the cylinder. *a²,* Chamber containing the suction-valves, and to which chamber are connected *a³, a³,* Suction pipes to which the hose is attached by screws in the usual manner, and which may be closed by the ordinary screw-cap. The delivering valves and passages at the top of the cylinder are similar to those just described, but the valve-chamber communicates directly with

B—Air vessel of a globular form, made of copper. *b, b,* Delivery pipes to which the pressure hose is attached. When only one jet is required, the opposite pipe may be closed by a screw cap, as usual. The piston or bucket of the force-pump to be provided with double leather packing; the piston-rod to be made of copper; the gland and stuffing box to be made of brass.

C— Boiler, constructed on the principle of the ordinary locomotive boiler, and containing 27 tubes of $1\frac{1}{2}$ inch diameter. The top of the steam chamber and the horizontal part of the boiler to be covered with wood, to prevent the radiation of heat. *c*, Fire door. *c*¹, Ash pan, consisting of a square box attached below the furnace, and having a small door in front. *c*², Square box attached to the end of the boiler, enclosing the exit of the tubes. The hot air from the tubes received by this box is passed off through *c*³, Smoke pipe, carried up through either of the spaces D, making a half-spiral turn round the air

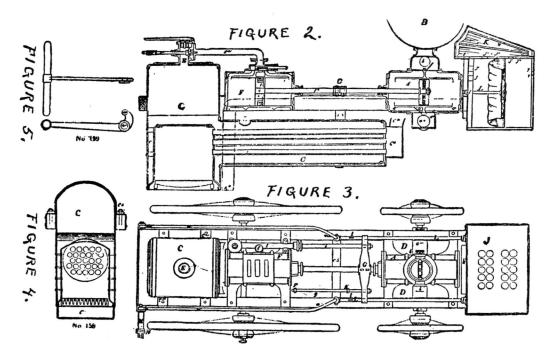

SECTIONAL VIEW OF ERICSSON'S ENGINE.

vessel, and terminating in the form of a serpent or a dragon, to avoid the unsightly appearance of an abrupt vertical termination. *c*⁴, Brackets of wrought iron, riveted to the upright part of the boiler, and bolted to the carriage frame. *c*⁵, Wrought iron stay, also bolted to the carriage frame, for supporting the horizontal part of the boiler.

E— Cylindrical box attached to the top of the steam chamber, containing *e*, Conical steam valve, and also *e*¹, Safety valve. *e*², Screw with handle connected to the steam valve for admitting or shutting off the steam. *e*³, Induction pipe, for conveying steam to

F— Steam cylinder, provided with steam passages and slide valve, of the usual construction, and secured to the carriage frame in similar manner to the force pump. *f*, Eduction pipe, for carrying off the steam into the atmosphere. *f*¹, Piston, provided with metallic packing (on Barton's plan). f^2, Piston rod of steel, attached to the piston rod of the force pump by means of

G — Cross head of wrought iron, into which both piston rods are inserted and secured by keys. *g*, Tappet-rod attached to the crosshead, for moving the slide-valve of the steam cylinder by means of g^1, g^1, Nuts which may be placed in any position on the tappet-rod.

H — Spindle of wrought iron, working in two bearings attached to the cover of the steam cylinder, the end thereof having fixed to it. *h*, Lever, moved or struck ultimately by the nuts g^1, g^1. h^1, Lever, fixed to the middle part of the spindle *H*, for moving the steam valve rod.

I — Force-pump for supplying the boiler, constructed with spindle valves on the ordinary plan ; the suction-pipe thereof to communicate with the valve chamber of the water cylinder, and the delivering pipe to be connected with the horizontal part of the boiler. *i*, Plunger of force-pump, to be made of gun-metal or copper, and attached to the crosshead *G*.

J — Blowing apparatus, consisting of a square wooden box, with panelled sides, in which is made to work *j*, Square piston, made of wood, joined to the sides of said box by leather. j^1, Circular holes or openings through the sides, for admitting atmospheric air into the box ; these holes being covered on the inside by pieces of leather or India rubber cloth to act as valves. j^2, are similar holes through the top of the box, for passing off the air at each stroke of the piston into

K — Receiver or regulator, which has *k*, Movable top, made of wood, joined by leather to the upper part of the box ; a thin sheet of lead to be attached thereto, for keeping up a certain compression of air in the regulator. k^1, Box or passage made of sheet iron, attached to the blowing apparatus, and having an open communication with the regulator at k^2. To this passage is connected a conducting pipe, as marked by dotted lines in figure 2, for conveying the air from the receiver into the ash-pan under the furnace of the boiler, at k^2; this conducting pipe passes along the inside of the carriage frame, on either side.

L, L — Two parallel iron rods, to which the piston of the blowing apparatus is attached. These rods work through guide-brasses *l, l*, and they may be attached to the crosshead *G*, by keys at l^1, l^1. The holes at the ends of the crossheads for admitting these rods, are sufficiently large to allow a free movement whenever it is desirable to work the blowing apparatus independently of the engine.

M — Spindle of wrought iron, placed transversely, and working in two bearings fixed under the carriage frame. To this spindle are fixed, *m, m*, two crank-levers, which by means of m^1, m^1, two connecting rods, will give motion to the piston-rods *L, L*, by inserting the hooks m^2, m^2, into the eyes at the ends of the said piston-rods.

N — Crank-lever, fixed at the ends of spindle *M*, which by means of

O — Crank-pin, fixed in the carriage wheel, and also

P — Connecting-rod, will communicate motion to the blowing apparatus, whenever the carriage is in motion, and the above parts duly connected.

n — Pin fixed in lever *N* placed at such distance from the centre of spindle *M*, that it will fit the hole n^1 of the lever shown in figure 5, while n^2 receives the end of spindle *M*. Whenever the blowing apparatus is to be worked by the engine or by manual force, the connecting rod *P* should be detached by means of the lock at *p*. The carriage frame should be made of oak, and plated with iron all over the outside and top; the top plate to have small recesses, to meet the brackets of the cylinders, as shown in the drawing. The lock of the carriage, axles and springs to be made as usual, only differing by having the large springs suspended *below* the axle. The carriage wheels to be constructed on the suspension principle; spokes and rim to be made of wrought iron very light.

With regard to the power of the engine represented by the drawing, it is estimated to be equal to 108 men.

"The experience which I have had," says Mr. Ericsson, "in the management of steam fire-engines, induces me to suggest, that the best way of keeping the engine always in readiness, is that of having a small boiler or hot water stove erected in the place where the engine is kept, and by means of a connecting pipe, with a screw joint, keep up heat in the engine boiler; the fire grate or flues of which should be kept very clean, with dry shavings, wood and coke carefully laid in the furnace, ready for ignition. A torch should always be at hand to ignite with at a moment's notice. The plan of keeping up a *constant* fire in the engine boiler is bad in practice, as it prevents the keeping the flues clean, and causes formation of sediment in the boiler, to say nothing of wear and tear; but which is still more important, perhaps, at the very moment of the word of fire being given, the furnace is covered with clinkers, or the engineer is busy cleaning it.

JOHN ERICSSON.

"The principal object of a Steam Fire-Engine being that of not depending on the power or diligence of a large number of men, one or two horses should always be kept in an adjoining stable for its transportation. To this fire-engine establishment the word of fire should be given, without intermediate orders; the horses being put to, the rod attached connecting the carriage wheel to the bellows, and the fuel ignited, the engine may on all ordinary occasions be at its destination, and in full operation within ten minutes."

Capt. John Ericsson will always be remembered for his designing of the iron war vessel *Monitor*. He died in New York City, on March 8, 1889.

WILLIAM L. LAY — 1851.

The name of William L. Lay, of Philadelphia, might have gone into history as an early builder of steam fire-engines had he received the support and encouragement that he deserved. But the volunteer firemen of those days could not be convinced that steam would lessen their labor and be far more powerful and efficient than the hand machines. They foresaw, rightly, that it would be the cause of the department being re-organized, and that the old way of doing fire duty would be changed, and discipline and strict rules adopted ; while at that time it was " Go as you please," " Hit a head wherever you can see one." The one that could drink the most was considered the best man. Rioting in large cities was nothing uncommon. There have been instances where hundreds of men were involved in mortal combat at firemen's riots, and not only were spanners and axes used as weapons, but firearms also. They called it sport and excitement ; and I do not doubt for a moment that it was. But they had had their day and the time had come for a change. They fought hard against it, and died in the harness ; and it was all for the best.

In the year 1851, Mr. William L. Lay invented and produced plans for a steam fire-engine to be worked by gas or steam. The inventor tried to sell an interest to parties who would try to introduce them ; but he was unsuccessful on account of the refusal of the volunteer firemen to have anything to do with steamers.

The plans provided for a self-propelling engine. The frame was straight, extending beyond the wheels (which were of iron) both front and rear. The boiler was vertical and tubular, and was placed on the centre of the frame, between the forward and rear wheels. It was intended that when the machine was in the engine house, the boiler should contain a sufficient quantity of water, and, at the same time, be charged with carbolic acid gas by suitable apparatus, until it contained sufficient to work the engine for ten minutes ; in which time, steam could be raised to take its place. The furnace door was on the off side of the boiler. The smoke stack was of the telescopic style and could be raised and lowered at pleasure. The boiler was equipped with whistle, lever, safety valve, etc. The steam cylinders were on either side of the engine, connected to the middle of the frame, and were calculated to be six horse power. Steam was admitted by a lever throttle. From the crosshead slide on the piston-rod was attached a connecting rod which propelled the engine by being connected with the rear wheels. Directly under the hind axle was the force-pump of a rotary pattern ; and it was intended that after the engine arrived at a fire, by working a combination of levers, the rear part of the engine would be lifted clear of the ground, and the hind wheels would then take the place of balance wheels, while the axle would work the pump by cog gearing attached to the

(11)

inside of the axle of the driving wheels. Directly under the boiler was a large feed water tank, to which was attached a blower to be used for a forced draft. The steering gear consisted of a vertical shaft with a large wheel on top. On the lower end of the shaft was a pinion, gearing into a segmental rack to guide the forward wheels, and make them turn easily. Below the steering-wheel was a circular head with indentations around it to receive a catch-rod ; which was pressed into the indentations by a spring below to keep the pinion of the steering apparatus secure from moving, when required. At the rear of the boiler was a large reel, capable of carrying a large amount of hose.

The whole weight was calculated to be about one and one half tons (3000 lbs.) but, if it had been constructed, the chances are that it would have weighed much more.

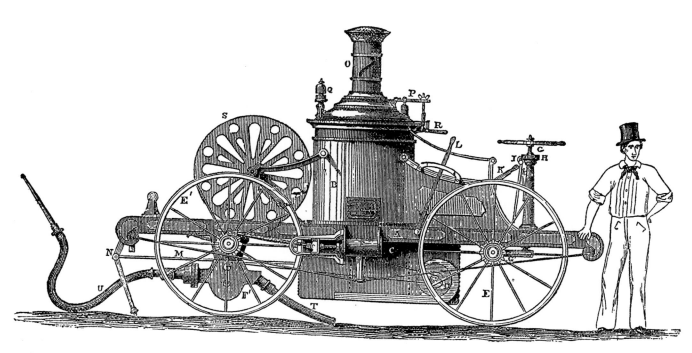

WILLIAM L. LAY'S DESIGN OF ENGINE.

LATTA — 1852.

To Moses Latta, of Cincinnati, Ohio, belongs the honor of inventing the first *successful* Steam Fire-Engine.

Previous to 1852, the city of Cincinnati had volunteer organizations and hand-engines. The means of conquering fires were inefficient. Immense losses of property occurred and scenes of disorder and violence were enacted. There was, in consequence, a desire felt by the people for better arrangements, both as to apparatus and operators. The public mind began to ripen for a paid fire department, and with the idea of a department of disciplined men, was naturally associated that of introducing steam into service in throwing water. Happily, the mechanical genius of the city was, at the same time, developing a boiler which would make steam fire-engines an inevitable success. The desideratum was a boiler capable of generating steam so rapidly as to render the steam engine as *prompt* as it would be *powerful* in a service requiring both qualities. The boiler was devised and constructed by mechanics of Cincinnati. The mechanical genius of the world had not previously achieved a machine at once portable, of adequate steaming qualities and powerful enough to throw the required volume of water. Cincinnati has the honor of having produced the desired mechanism.

In the year 1852, the first experimental steam fire-engine was built, and was tested before the City Council, on March 2, 1852; and it was proven, to their entire satisfaction, that a steam fire-engine could be built to extinguish fires. This first, or experimental engine, had 8-in. steam cylinder, 2-ft. stroke, with a 4-in. Farnam hand-engine pump. The boiler was constructed of coiled gas-pipe, encased in sheet iron, and the wheels, etc., were taken from an old hook and ladder truck. Steam was raised from cold water in 4 min. 10 sec. from the time smoke issued from the stack, and water was forced through 350 feet of hose to the distance of 130 ft. The experiment was convincing, and the City Council contracted with Latta to build an engine, which he immediately proceeded to do; and the result was that he placed before the public the first *successful* steam fire-engine in the world. This engine was named " Joe Ross," and was appropriately named for " Uncle Joe Ross," as he was familiarly called. He died in July, 1875.

It was he who induced the City Council to appropriate $5000 for the same. The engine was a ponderous self propeller with two rear wheels and one on front, which acted as a steering wheel. The boiler was square and upright and was called the gunpowder boiler. It was so called because steam was generated by flashing cold water into a hot boiler. There were two horizontal cylinders, one on each side; the pumps being in front of the cylinders and driven direct. The engines were made to couple, when required, with the driving wheels, which were at the rear of the engine. The weight was

22,000 lbs., and required four horses, which were ridden artillery fashion, besides the propelling power which the machine furnished.

The engine was tested at the corner of Front St. and Broadway. The suction hose was thrown into a cistern and water was thrown in 7 min. through 3-in. hose with a 1½-in. nozzle to the distance of 225 ft., and, to the astonishment of thousands of people present, water was thrown through 2, 4 and 6 lines of hose at the same time, each stream

"CITIZENS' GIFT" ENGINE OF CINCINNATI.
Built by Latta.

capable of doing good fire service. The engineer who ran her was Finley Latta, brother of the inventor. The engine was accepted and placed in service Jan. 1, 1853, under the charge of a permanent company.

Thus, the first paid fire company to operate with the untiring energy of steam, was brought into existence, the first in any age or country. While this engine was in the course of construction, a stranger called at the works of Mr. Greenwood and was allowed the privilege, then seldom granted, of going into the workroom where the inventor was at work. It was a long, high room, the walls on the east side being hung with drawings of the engine. Beneath the drawings ran a long work-bench, and at this stood a man; a very diminutive specimen of humanity, short and spare, stoop-shouldered, even to deformity. He had a square, white-paper hat on his head, and was busy measuring something. While looking at him, the stranger saw that his head redeemed his poor body; for it was massive, and the eyes had in them the light of genius. In a moment he turned and asked, " Did Mr. Greenwood give you permission to come in here?" The stranger replied, " He did, he told me to come and see how the engine was getting on."

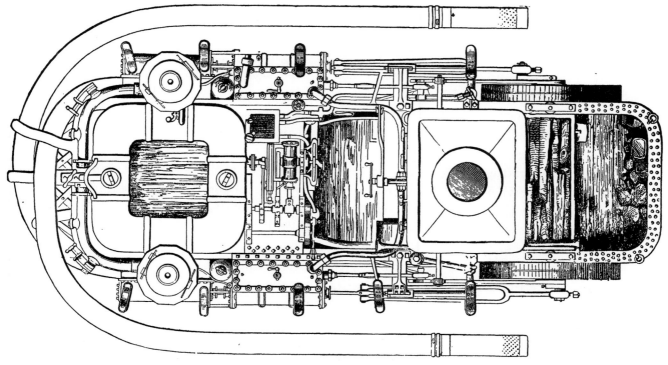

TOP VIEW OF THE "CITIZENS' GIFT."

" Ah! Very well," said the inventor, " very well! My name is Latta, Moses Latta, and as you come from him, you shall see what few see. Can you in any way or to any extent understand the drawings on the wall?" The stranger confessed that he could not. " Well! it is very simple, let me explain. The engine is intended to throw, at any time, eight streams of water; four from each side, whenever the water can be obtained in sufficient quantity for that number. It is intended, of course, to take the engine to the scene of the fire with horses—about four. As the engine starts out, the furnace is fired up, and, ordinarily, by the time it would arrive at the fire, steam will be up and the engine ready for service. Eight of these large streams, forced out on a fire, with the pressure we shall be able to command, will drown any fire. Even four of them, well directed, will be of wonderful value. But," added Mr. Latta, " the trouble is that there is no certainty that this, or any other steam fire-engine, will ever be allowed to work at a fire. You are, probably, not aware how bitter is the feeling of the volunteer firemen against this engine. They say it shall never throw a stream of water on a fire in this city; and I sometimes fear that I shall never live to see this grand idea brought into the service of the world. The recent riots here show what a mob can do in our city. My steps are dogged. Spies are continually on my track. I am worried with all sorts of anonymous communications, threatening me with all sorts of ills and evils unless I drop work on this engine, and pronounce it a failure." The old man's eyes flashed as he said : " I'll never give up! I'll build it, and there are men enough in this city to see that it has a fair trial; and it shall have it. When it is finished, it will be heard from at the first fire, and woe to those who stand in its way."

As the time approached for the trial of the engine, the volunteer firemen were in a ferment. It would never do to destroy the engine before it had had a trial ; and to destroy it after a successful exhibit of its powers was made, would be equally useless. So it was understood that no demonstration, pro or con, would be made on it until it should come to a fire, when it was to be rendered useless and all who had a hand in its working were to be rendered useless also.

The public trial came off. The engine far exceeded in efficiency anything that had been claimed for it, either by its inventor or by its backers; and a feeling of satisfaction swept over the city at the knowledge that such a great auxiliary power was in their midst to fight fires. Still it was known, or generally believed, that its first appearance at a fire would be the signal for as bloody a riot as ever disgraced the city. The volunteer fire-department was there, as almost everywhere else, a political ring, far more efficient, under ordinary circumstances, at the polls than at the fire ; and its members, to a man, were selected for their influence at the voting precincts, and for their ability to make the contents of the ballot-box, when it was emptied, show, by a large majority, their man ahead — no matter what kind of ballots had gone into it. Then, if this steamer was of any account, it would ruin and break up, not only the hand-engine companies, but their friends and backers and the manufacturers who built hand-engines.

At last the crisis came. One night an alarm rang out for a fire in a great warehouse on Third Street near Main. A moment or two elapsed to the listeners on Main Street above Fourth, and then down came the great steam fire-engine, four mammoth gray horses in front of it, at a gallop ; the smoke streaming from its stack, the fire flashing from its grates. Its ponderous wheels ground the cobble-stones into powder as they struck them ; and as the great monster went down the hill, people woke as out of a trance and started after it. The engine was brought in front of the block and soon afterward stream after stream shot from it. The houses were among the most valuable in the city, and were stored with costly goods. The time had come ; the engine was there. Four streams had been thrown on when the cry, " The hose is cut," rang out. Then the melée began. But the citizens were stronger than the volunteer firemen ; and after a struggle the steamer drowned out the fire and was taken home.

The next morning Moses Latta awoke to find himself famous ; and the action of the appreciative citizens of Cincinnati soon put him in a position where his genius was made more available to the world. On the sixth day of December, 1855, the " Joe Ross " was

CROSS SECTION PUMP AND STEAM CYLINDER ENGINE.
Built by A. B. & E. Latta.

taken out for a trial. She had worked but a short time when the leading hose burst and the machine was shut down ; whereupon, the boiler exploded with great force, killing the engineer, Mr. John Winterbottom, and injuring several others. The accident was caused by the fire-box not being properly stayed. At the time of the explosion, the boiler had a steam pressure of 180 lbs.

The steamer of to-day has little in common with it, except the fact that it is built to effect the same purpose as was Latta's engine. But that was the germ of all those which now, at the tap of the electric bell, seem to hitch themselves to the horses and tear along our streets.

In the spring of 1854, when the city had but one steamer (the " Uncle Joe Ross "), the sum of $13,400 was raised by voluntary contribution for the purchase and equipment of another large engine. This machine was appropriately named " Citizens' Gift " and was a splendid machine ; with a three-wheel click, double 11 in. cylinders, 6⅝ pumps, square, upright boiler and weighed 11,820 lbs. Her record was 3 min. 10 sec. on raising steam. She threw a horizontal stream through 2½ in. hose, 1½ in. nozzle, the great distance of 297 ft.

The price paid for this engine was $10,000. For several years, the firm of A. B. & E. Latta did quite an extensive business, with little or no opposition. In 1863, they sold out their business to Lane & Bodley, who built seven or eight machines from the old patterns and transferred the business in 1868 to the Ahrens Manufacturing Co.

ABEL SHAWK — 1855.

Abel Shawk of Cincinnati built his first Steam Fire-Engine in 1855, and afterwards built four others.

The boiler of his first engine had a fire-box $3\frac{1}{2}$ feet by $4\frac{1}{2}$ feet high, with arched top and containing a continuous series of small, horizontal, parallel tubes. In connection with this was a horizontal cylinder 10 inches by $2\frac{1}{2}$ inches, placed near the ground and unequally divided by a vertical, transverse diaphragm. In the larger part, near the upright case, was another continuous series of small tubes, the space around them being connected with the end of the first named series of tubes. The other end of this first series, and one end of the second series, were in connection with the force-pump. On lighting the fire, the first series of tubes became heated; the water being injected into them was converted into steam, and, entering the cylindrical case, heated the water injected or ran over into the second series converting it into steam, and thus supplying the required amount to run the engine. The farthest end of the cylindrical case received the water from the pump, which had one suction inlet and eight hose gates. The steam cylinder was $11\frac{3}{8}$ inches by 25 inches, and was placed horizontally on this case, and next to the boiler. The pump was $7\frac{3}{8}$ inches by 25 inches, and was in front of the steam cylinder, on a line with the same and directly connected with it. The piston-rod had a three armed crosshead, the two lower ones working the feed-pumps, which were placed on the side of the steam cylinder. The top one worked a small valve which admitted steam on either end of a small cylinder, to the piston-rod of which was affixed the main steam-valve, thus allowing the main piston to complete its stroke before reversing.

In the winter of 1855–56, the city of St. Louis had some weeks of intensely cold weather, and the Mississippi River had a natural bridge, so strong that the Shawk engine was taken across on the ice. This was the pioneer steam fire-engine on the west bank of the Mississippi; but it was too heavy and cumbrous for convenient working (a great fault with all early steam fire-engines) and did not come into use.

But little was ever heard of the Shawk engine; and it is believed that he, like several other builders of steamers, got discouraged and soon gave up that branch of the business. He was quite a noted hand-engine builder. One of his hand machines is credited with having made the remarkable horizontal throw of 273 feet. Mr. Shawk was, for a short time, a partner with Latta, the famous steam fire-engine builder of Cincinnati.

JOSEPH L. LOWRY — 1855.

Among the early pioneers to produce steam fire-engines can be found the name of Mr. Joseph L. Lowry, a mechanical engineer of Pittsburgh, Pa. In the year 1839 or '40, a controversy arose in that city as to which hand-engine would throw the most water. Mr. Lowry became very much interested in the subject, and, while sitting in church one day, conceived the idea of retaining and throwing water with the pressure of a plug hydrant ; and to demonstrate his plan, he got the "President," a suction engine, belonging to the sister city of Allegheny, which threw 110 feet without men working it and 200 feet with the men working the brakes.

Sometime between 1842 and '45, he discovered and made a direct acting engine and thought it would make an excellent steam fire-engine. But the matter rested until 1854. In 1855, he received from the Board of Underwriters of Pittsburgh a contract for an engine which he completed in the same year. All steam fire engines built previous to this were constructed horizontally ; but in this machine, the pump and steam cylinder were placed vertical, direct acting with crank motion. The pump measured $11\frac{5}{16}$ inches in diameter with 24 inch stroke of piston — steam cylinder 16 inches in diameter, 24 inch stroke. The boiler was 43 inches in diameter and 8 feet 4 inches in length ; was made of heavy $\frac{1}{4}$ inch iron, capable of standing a steam pressure of 200 lbs. It contained 253 flues, 2 inches in diameter and 4 feet long. With a pressure of 115 lbs. of steam, it threw 1,500 gallons of water through a $2\frac{1}{2}$ inch nozzle 189 feet in one minute, and through a 2 inch nozzle 215 feet, keeping it up from 30 to 40 minutes. This engine could carry 13 men, weighed 5 tons and required four horses to haul it. It was used with good success for nine months, but owing to there not being a sufficient supply of water, it was discarded.

Only one more of these engines was built, which was a smaller size than his first, and was completed in 1857. The pump of this machine measured 10 inches in diameter, steam cylinder 14 inches. The boiler contained 250 tubes, 3 feet long. The weight was $4\frac{1}{2}$ tons. This engine, with a steam pressure of 100 lbs., threw 9 streams 200 feet ; and one stream, through a $1\frac{3}{4}$ inch nozzle, with only 60 lbs. steam pressure, 260 feet.

SILSBY—1856.

The Silsby Manufacturing Co. of Seneca Falls, N. Y., is now the oldest Steam Fire-Engine building company in the country. They were pioneers and produced their first engine in 1856. Since then they have built over one thousand machines.

I have no desire in this connection to indulge in boastful praise of the Silsby engine, though I feel justified in pointing with pride to the unparalleled record that it has made for itself. Constructed upon entirely original and novel principles, for years it was condemned by theorists, by machinists and engineers who were wedded to the piston or reciprocating system of engines and pumps, while the pumps and steam-cylinders of the Silsby were known as the rotary motion, Mr. Birdsall Holly's patent. It is true that the rotary pump of years ago had its faults; and if they were not continually looked after, would be the condemning of any engine; but they were adopted by a firm that was bound to perfect the pump and cylinder if it lay in the power of mechanical ingenuity to do so; well knowing that, when perfected, a rotary motion is far superior to a piston or sliding motion; for it not only does away with pump-valves, which are very apt to get out of order, but it also reduces the friction to a great extent as there are no cross head-slides or link block-bearings.

For many years they continued to improve their pumps, taking out patent after patent; and were at last rewarded for their years of labor by overcoming all the faults that, years ago, were the cause of many condemning the rotary principle. So, to-day, it is acknowledged by experts who are not prejudiced to be the best fire-pump in the world.

The " Island Works," owned and run by the Silsby Manufacturing Co. of Seneca Falls, N. Y., were established in 1845, by Mr. Horace C. Silsby. He was born in the state of Connecticut in the year 1817. The island embraces about five (5) acres. The buildings, from time to time, have been enlarged to accommodate the increasing business, and at the present cover almost the whole island.

To recount the history of this pioneer in the business of supplying the world with machinery capable of doing work never imagined by the most sanguine of inventors fifty years ago, we must go back to the year 1856, when the first Silsby steamer was built. The firm, at that time, was known as " Silsby, Mynderse & Co.," consisting of Horace C. Silsby, Edward Mynderse and John Shoemaker. Messrs. Silsby and Mynderse are still alive and reside in Seneca Falls, but Mr. Shoemaker died some years ago.

The weight of this experimental engine was about 9,500 lbs., and as viewed from to-day's standpoint of excellence of workmanship, it was indeed a curiosity; and yet, within its crude lines, it contained all the points of excellence which, by modification, have been so strongly brought to the surface in the engines of later build by this most successful firm. This engine of 1856 resembled as much a Mississippi steamboat as it would one of our modern steamers. The boiler was horizontal, of the locomotive style, with large steam dome. On top of the boiler were the steam cylinders and pumps which

FIRST SILSBY STEAM FIRE-ENGINE, 1856.

were both of the rotary pattern. On top of the boiler was also a platform on which the engineer stood while working the engine. On the off hind wheel on the felloe was a gear which worked an air blower in the pan of the engine while on the way to a fire, thus furnishing a forced draft for the boiler. She was named "Neptune," and was exhibited at the Crystal Palace at New York City in 1856. At the trial, with a pressure of 60 lbs. of steam, four streams were thrown over 200 ft., and six streams 150 ft. each, using 1⅛ in. nozzles. This engine was only experimental and was never sold or placed in service, but was broken up a short time after being made.

At the time the "Neptune" was built, the firm had in their employ Mr. M. R. Clapp, who, later on, was the originator of the Clapp and Jones' engine, also Birdsall Holly, the inventor of the rotary steam cylinder and pump that was first used, and has been ever since used, in the Silsby engine. Mr. Clapp was also the inventor of the drop-tube boiler. Both of these men shortly afterwards retired from connection with the Silsby

SILSBY PISTON ENGINE.

Co., Mr. Holly going to Lockport, N. Y., and Mr. Clapp to New York City. Both have since died. Mr. Mynderse retired from the business shortly after the first engine was built, which left Mr. Horace C. Silsby the sole proprietor.

His next steamer that was built was quite an improvement on the first, and was sold to the city of Chicago in 1857 for $5,000, and it was in successful use in that city for a great many years. It was named "Long John," and was finally destroyed in the tunnel in collision with another engine or some other vehicle. The horizontal boiler was used until 1860, when the plans were changed and a vertical boiler was adopted.

Every year of the existence of this firm has shown that they have always had an eye open for improvements, and at the present time their engines are rated A No. 1. They build seven sizes which are models of beauty. Their Extra First weighs 7,500 lbs. Capacity 1,100 gallons per minute.

First size, Weight 6,800 lbs.	.	.	.	.	Capacity 950 galls.
Second "	" 6,300 "	.	.	.	.	" 800 "
Third "	" 5,700 "	.	.	.	.	" 700 "
Fourth "	" 5,300 "	.	.	.	.	" 600 "
Fifth "	" 4,800 "	.	.	.	.	" 500 "
Sixth "	" 4.000 "	.	.	.	.	" 400 "

MODERN SILSBY ENGINE.

The greatest authentic distance to which a stream has been thrown by the Silsby steamer was 364 ft., at Reading, Pa., Sept. 24, 1881.

The steam cylinder of the Silsby engine consists of two rotary cams which work together within an elliptical steam-tight case. Live steam is admitted to the bottom of the case, and pressing apart the long teeth, it revolves the two cams in its passage and exhausts from the top into the stack and feed water heater. Each cam is provided with teeth adapted to mesh in recesses in the other, so that a tight joint is maintained between them, and steam is prevented from passing directly upward to the exhaust. The cams have their sides turned to fit the heads of the case, and are so adjusted that, while being steam-tight, ample allowance is made for contraction and expansion due to cold and heat. Any little wear there may be after years of service can be easily taken up in a very short time.

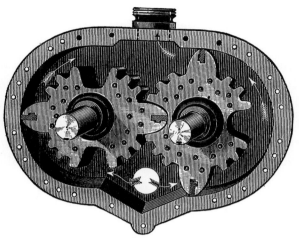

SILSBY ROTARY STEAM CYLINDER.

In the ends of the long teeth of the cams are placed removable packing-strips which are forced out into contact with the walls of the cylinder by springs. These packing-strips can be taken out in a few minutes through openings in the sides of the case and set out, it being on the ends of these that the only wear comes.

The construction of the pump is the same as the steam cylinder, excepting that there are three long teeth in each cam, instead of two, insuring a steady flow of water. One shaft of the pump is coupled to the corresponding shaft of the cylinder, there being outside gears on both cylinder and pump to steady the motion of the cams and equalize the pressure. The water ways being large, direct and unobstructed, anything liable to enter the suction will pass through the pump without injury or interruption to its working, and there being an entire absence of valves, leaves, sticks, saw-dust, mud and other foreign substances can be safely worked with this machine.

The motion of the pump being equable, continuous and rotary, no blows are given to the water, which enters and leaves in one steady flow, and there is, therefore, no irregular motion to the stream, nor uneven or pulsating pressure on the hose. The pump does not require priming, and will, when started, immediately draught water up to 29 feet vertical lift, without the use of check valve. It will also force water and do good fire duty through 3000 feet of hose or upwards, without danger of bursting the hose. The steam cylinder and pump being on one shaft, the action is direct and continuous, and there being no loss of power between cylinder and pump, fire duty can be accomplished with low steam pressure.

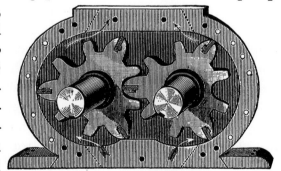

SILSBY ROTARY PUMP.

The machine also stands perfectly still, even when doing its heaviest fire duty ; so still, in fact, that a glass of water may be placed on one of the wheels and not a drop be spilled. There is also an entire absence of friction on the hose. As will be seen, in this cylinder and pump, the working parts are few in number and consist entirely of metal, no leather or rubber entering into their construction.   From its simplicity, it is not likely to get out of order, and any one of ordinary intelligence can very soon learn to run and manage it.   The construction of the boiler is shown in the accompanying cut.

In the fire box hang circulating water tubes arranged in concentric circles and tightly screwed into the crown sheet.   These tubes are closed at their lower ends by means of wrought iron plugs welded in.   Within each tube is a thinner tube open at both ends.   The cooler water in the boiler descends through the thinner tube and is thus brought into the midst of the fire, where, mostly converted into steam, it ascends into the annular space between the inner and outer tubes.   The gases of combustion pass from the fire-box to the stack through smoke flues that are securely expanded at their lower ends into the crown sheet, and at their upper ends into the top head.   The circulation of water is so strong as to effectually prevent the accumulation of mud, scales, or other sedi-

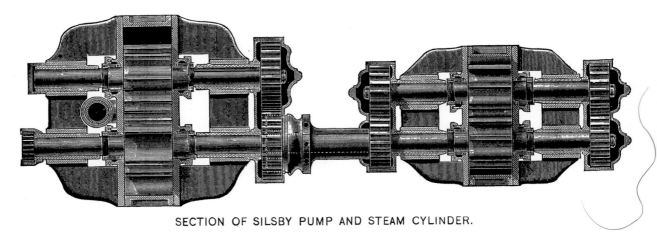

SECTION OF SILSBY PUMP AND STEAM CYLINDER.

ment in the drop flues or elsewhere in the boiler, depositing it in the water leg, from which it can be readily removed through suitable cleaning holes.

The steam, which is further heated and dried by the smoke flues, is taken from a copper pipe perforated on top, which encircles the steam space between the shell and smoke flues near their upper ends, thus insuring absolutely dry steam.   The draught is regulated by a variable exhaust, consisting of four outlets each controlled by a conical plug, the whole operated by a lever enabling the engineer to regulate the steam pressure. The rapid succession of discharges makes in effect a steady blast, which does not pull fire and thus endanger surrounding property by throwing live coals.   There being several outlets, there is also a very even pull of the blast upon the grate surface.

The ready accessibility of every part of the boiler for the purpose of making repairs is apparent, it not being necessary to tear the boiler to pieces.   The water tubes may be unscrewed and replaced in a few minutes and all the smoke flues may be readily got at by removing the dome.   The heating surface in water tubes, smoke flues, and fire-box walls being so large and effective, the steaming power of the boiler is immense.   Steam is generated from cold water in from three to five minutes; thus an effective fire stream is quickly forced.

The shell and fire box of this boiler are made of tough and strong homogeneous steel, having a tensile strength of 60,000 pounds to the square inch, and which will neither temper nor crystallize. The tubes are double the actually required strength. All holes in the sheets and heads are drilled, not punched. All joints are permanently tight. All heating surfaces being straight, they are easily kept clean on both sides, and those exposed to the direct action of the fire are covered with water. The boiler will burn either coal or wood, will not prime, and salt water can be used in it if necessary. The boiler can be fed from the main pump, but there is an independent feed pump, by which the boiler can be fed with hot water, and with fresh water while the machine is pumping salt water or that otherwise unfit for steaming.

The machine is provided with a special attachment whereby the feed water, supplied from a tank, is heated to a temperature of about 212 degrees

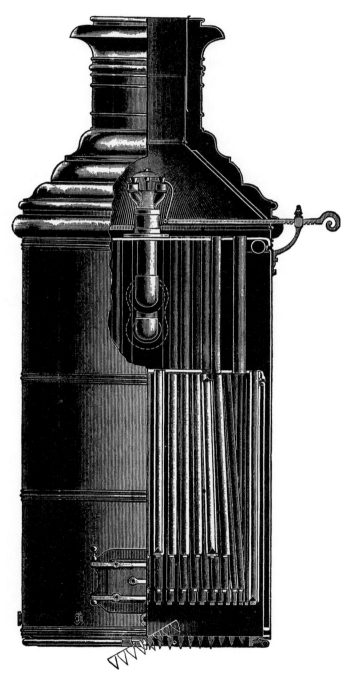

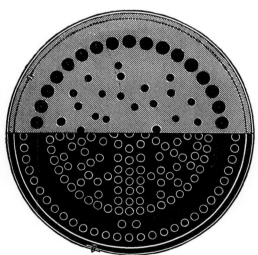

SECTION OF SILSBY BOILER.

MODERN SILSBY BOILER.

(F), using for this purpose exhaust steam from the cylinder. The packing pieces in the ends of the long teeth of the cams and their patented form of stuffing boxes, used in both steam cylinder and pump, are shown in the above cut. This stuffing box is self-adjusting, reduces friction, insures such absolute tightness that there is not a particle of leakage of either steam or water, and does away with the necessity of frequent re-packing. There is also a special patented form of boxing, entirely preventing over heating of the journals with any long-continued service or from neglect.

These machines are built "crane-neck" style, and are adapted to be drawn by horses only, or by either horses or men. The former are hung on platform springs in front and half elliptic springs in the rear, with brake operated by driver's foot. The latter are hung on spiral springs front and rear, and have a "combination pole," suitable for hand or horse draft, with driver's seat and drag rope and reel, the brake being operated from the fuel pan in rear.

A short time ago, this company consolidated with the following steam fire-engine builders: Ahrens of Cincinnati, Ohio, Button of Waterford, New York, and Clapp & Jones of Hudson, New York; and are now known as the "American Fire Engine Co."

LEE AND LARNED — 1856.

The firm of Lee & Larned commenced building steam fire-engines at the Novelty Works, New York City, in the year 1856.

Their machines were what were termed the "Mongrel" engines, on account of their having rotary pump and piston steam cylinder. Their engines were built to be drawn by horses or hand or self-propelling. One of the latter was used with success for some time by the Exempt Engine Co., of New York City. This engine was given her first trial at the "Bowling Green" one afternoon in November, 1858, before a large assemblage of citizens, a large majority of whom were firemen. The engine worked admirably and to the satisfaction of many officials and prominent men. The engine commenced working about half past two and continued in operation until four o'clock. The trial was highly satisfactory to every one. All sizes of nozzles were used, from 1 inch to an open butt of $2\frac{1}{2}$ inches. All persons on the ground expressed themselves satisfied that one steam fire engine, of the size of the one on exhibition, would be of more service, in case of a large fire, than a dozen hand-engines. The members of "Empire" Engine 42 took charge of the hose and pipe and attended to the working of the engine. They performed their duty well, and had sense enough to refrain from wetting the lookers-on unnecessarily.

This engine resembled a street locomotive, and was capable of propelling itself over any ordinary street or road. It was guided by the running gear of F. R. Fisher, whose steam carriage was attracting a great deal of attention in those days.

The frame or bed, of boiler and angle iron, was hung upon four strong springs running lengthwise, and one cross spring under the hinder axle. The two front springs, placed one above the other in the line of the centre of the carriage, took hold of a vertical spindle connected with the forward axle by a kind of universal joint, and having at the top a horizontal crank ; by turning which, by means of a winch and screw, the direction of the axle was controlled, and the carriage of the engine was steered with great facility and precision. The boiler was placed about half way between the forward and rear wheels and was vertical ; adjoining which, was an encasement where the engineer stood while running the engine.

The total weight was about five tons. Steam could be raised to a working pressure in from six to ten minutes. But it was intended that steam should be kept up at all times, so that the engine could start off at a minute's notice. When it reached a fire, the parallel rods were disconnected, which could be done in an instant ; and the power then acted upon the pump alone. The pump could discharge 6 gallons per revolution, and might be run with good effect, at any speed from 50 to 225 revolutions per minute. At

(29)

any ordinary rate of working, it would discharge from 600 to 700 gallons per minute through a single $1\frac{1}{2}$ inch nozzle, or its equivalent in smaller streams, giving a velocity sufficient for a horizontal throw of 200 feet or over.   This engine was handled by side ropes when taken out for this trial, but they were altogether unnecessary, as the steam power was all that was required, even in ascending the rising ground in Nassau Street from Maiden Lane to Fulton Street.   On the whole, the trial was a success, and the steam fire-engine movement lost nothing by this exhibition.

SELF-PROPELLER BUILT BY LEE & LARNED.

Shortly afterwards another trial was given this engine.   The test took place at the " Park."   She threw a stream through a $1\frac{5}{8}$ inch nozzle to the distance of 267 feet, with a 2 inch nozzle 232 feet, and through an open butt of $2\frac{1}{2}$ inches diameter 196 feet. The reader, if a man of experience, will, no doubt, say, " That is a lie or a misprint" ; but nevertheless, the judges claimed that they measured from the spot where the butt was held to the centre of the place where the main body of the water fell and the distance was 179 feet.

These self-propelling engines did not meet with general approval on account of their weight, and there were only two or three built.   However, the firm did quite an extensive business, and sold a great many of their lighter engines to be drawn by horse or hand.

The most noted engine built by this firm was "Manhattan, No. 8," of New York City. This engine had a vertical tubular boiler, 48 by 26 in., steam cylinder 7 by 8½ in., and could run about 400 strokes per minute. The pump was rotary (J. C. Cary's patent), the weight of the engine being 5,100 lbs. In 1863, quite a ripple of excitement was occasioned among the members of the New York Fire Department, by the reception of an invitation from the fire department of London, requesting New York to send to that city one of her steam engines for the purpose of competing with others at a public exhibition to be given at the Crystal Palace. "Manhattan, No. 8" was selected, and, in due time, arrived in London, in charge of Mr. Chas. Nichols, its foreman. Word soon came back to New York that Manhattan boys were not being treated honestly by their English friends. The story of Manhattan's troubles, briefly told, is as follows: —

On the day before the trial, the engine was brought to the Crystal Palace for the purpose of testing her, when an accident occurred. It seems that the Americans, on looking over the Crystal Palace grounds, did not discover that there were any hills. Foreman Nichols had passed his eye over the ground believing he was to take the route over which he walked ; so he prepared himself only for a gradual declivity. But, instead of going over this route, the New York boys were taken in an entirely different direction. Mr. Nichols and the engineer, Mr. Collins, took the tongue; but a Mr. Robbins, an English engineer, insisted upon taking the foreman's place, as he said he was acquainted with the route; and the request was granted. So the party started with about fifteen of the London fire brigade on the rope. Upon arriving at the top of the hill, some eight or ten of the Londoners left, when the engine commenced descending what was apparently a small hill. It was abrupt and tortuous, and almost within a few feet from the decline, there was an angle of about thirty degrees. The machine becoming unmanageable, and with lack of sufficient men at the hold-back ropes to keep her in check (there being only five of the London brigade left), her weight and speed were too much, and all power of direction was lost. The result was that she struck a tree and fell almost bottom upwards, knocking off her fore-carriage, breaking her fly-wheel, and, of course, materially injuring and wrenching the whole engine.

With full American pluck, the laddies determined to put her in order, if possible, for the trial of the next day. It was a heavy load to lift. Imagine Fifty One Hundred-weight of American machinery, after such a violent collision, to be lifted and put in order within twelve hours. But with energy, men and rope, the American boys did it; and got their engine to the grounds so that they might not forfeit the $50 for entrance fee. On the grounds, Engineer Collins at once examined the machinery of the Manhattan. Externally she appeared, except the fly-wheel, to be all right; but he was fearful of some internal injury which could not be discovered. The committee on prizes and others were afraid of the Manhattan bursting her boiler; and would not allow her to be tried until her boiler was re-tested. Capt. Shaw, of the London fire brigade, thought it unsafe and not best for the American engine to enter. But, having crossed the Atlantic for that purpose, Foreman Nichols and Engineer Collins said: "We will try her, if it kills us." So they re-tested the boiler, and found it in good condition; and, though otherwise crippled, the English machinists admired her greatly. Mr. Lee, the patentee, being on the ground, at once offered to bet £100 that she would win; thus showing that he had not only great faith in his own ingenuity, but also in the Novelty Works that built her.

The test was most severe. They were compelled to draft through 30 ft. of suction hose and play through almost 500 ft. of leading hose up an inclined plane of from 20 to 40 ft., and then the jet was to play into another ascent of 60 ft. On the start, they lifted their water quicker than any other engine on the ground. But, unfortunately, the Manhattan fly-wheel gave out and it was found that the machinery was injured, and it became necessary to stop at once.

MANHATTAN NO. 8, NEW YORK CITY
Built by Lee & Larned.

The report of the trial in the *London Times* contained the usual slurs, which, at that time, the journal was accustomed to cast upon everything American. The following extracts were taken from the *Times.*

"It must be understood that the American Steam Fire-Engines are as much behind the steam fire-engines of other countries, as that most pretentious Political Association called the 'New York Fire-Brigade' is behind any fire-brigade in Europe in real usefulness.

"Yesterday the 'Manhattan,' which was seriously injured by turning over, when brought upon the ground Tuesday, was tried in the presence of His Royal Highness. It was scarcely fair to try this engine at all, but the American gentlemen themselves wished it, and steam was got up accordingly. Before it pumped long, however, it was found to be too much injured to work with safety, as a crack, which the fly-wheel had received when it fell over, began to spread so fast that the machine had to be stopped at once."

Any comment on this criticism would be simply superfluous. My readers can form their own opinion of English fair play.

Shortly after, the " Manhattan," with her disappointed followers, arrived back in New York, where an enthusiastic reception was given her. The engine which was sent across the sea to beat the Britishers, and got beaten and broken, was pretty well inspected all along the route. She looked as if she had been used badly. There was an appearance of defection about her that would lead one versed in the peculiarities of fire-engines to suppose that she had either misbehaved in some way, or been treated shabbily. She seemed to shuffle along with a side gait very much like a chap who had been keeping late hours and had drawn his hat over his eyes that the early sun might not get a peep at them. In fact, she was not the bright " Manhattan " that had left New York but a short time before. It might have been that the old lady was sea-sick and had not recovered her strength, or that she had lost her character; or it might have been shame that she had not a big prize to show. However, on the occasion referred to, nearly one-half of the fire department turned out to do her honor.

The building of Lee & Larned steam fire-engines was discontinued about the last part of the '60's. Mr. Wellington Lee, the inventor, was a Civil and Mechanical Engineer. He was born at Sheridan, in Chautauqua Co., N. Y. He was given a contract to suppress all fires in the city of New Orleans, and built a number of his engines for this purpose ; trained and equipped a corps of men, and when the war broke out, had an efficient department in working order. The contract was for five years ; and only six months of that time had elapsed, when hostilities broke out, and Mr. Lee came home, leaving his property behind. He was an intense Union man and an enthusiastic patriot. His lameness prevented him from taking active part in the struggle, but he sent as many men into the field as his means would allow. Mr. Lee was a warm-hearted, generous man, esteemed by all who knew him, and was mourned by an extensive circle of friends. He died at his residence, No. 15 Laight St., New York City, in 1881, in the sixty-fifth year of his age.

REANIE AND NEAFIE — 1857.

The firm of Reanie & Neafie of Philadelphia was the most successful firm of steam fire-engine builders in the Keystone State. The designer of this unique machine was Mr. Joseph L. Parry. Mr. Parry claimed to be a thoroughbred American. He was born in Montgomery County, Pennsylvania, where his father and grandfather lived before him. Mr. Parry was a Quaker. He wore no beard, and the face, except for a few deep lines, was the same in appearance when he died, July 16, 1894, as it was away back in 1857 when he gave to the world as powerful and practical a steam fire-engine as had ever been invented.

Mr. Parry, at first, took his plans to John Agnew, the celebrated builder of double-deck hand-engines ; but he could not be persuaded to build steamers at that time, a thing which he much regretted shortly after. In 1857, the Philadelphia Hose Co., No. 1, learned that he had drawings for such a machine, and the following committee was appointed from among its members to raise a fund of $3,500 to construct an engine after his design: Cornelius Tiers Myers, John E. Neall, John K. Kane, Samuel V. Merrick, William D. Sherrerd, T. S. Cromboiger and Richard Vaux, Mayor of Philadelphia. By persistent efforts, the money was obtained ; and Mr. Parry superintended the construction of the engine at the works of Reanie & Neafie, where he was employed.

The contract was to raise steam in 15 minutes and throw a stream 190 feet with $1\frac{1}{4}$ inch nozzle. The engine was given its first trial on the wharf of its builders on Christmas day, 1857. It was a pronounced success, being able to throw a continuous stream 275 feet horizontally with 125 pounds steam pressure, using a $1\frac{1}{4}$ inch nozzle ; and 230 feet perpendicular. Steam was raised in 9 minutes. Afterwards, at Coates Street Wharf, Schuylkill, she threw 296 feet with $1\frac{3}{8}$ inch nozzle.

This old engine is still in use, being owned by the Philadelphia Fire Patrol. It is the pet of the men employed in this particular branch of the fire service, and is stationed on Arch Street, near Fifth.

The old engine presents a curious appearance when compared with one of the modern nickel-plated or highly burnished machines of to-day. The principal use at present is as a pump to empty cellars after a fire is extinguished ; but in an emergency, the old machine could do effective work.

The following are the dimensions of this old settler ; which is, without doubt, the oldest steam fire-engine in existence. It was what was termed a first class engine, and weighed 7,455 lbs., without fuel or water. The boiler was vertical, 30 inch diameter, with 187 iron smoke tubes, each 49 inches long and $1\frac{1}{2}$ inches internal diameter ; square fire-box, cold feed. The hind axle was cranked 10 inches. The engine was what was known as a single engine, as it had but one pump and one steam cylinder which lay horizontally on a cylindrical frame which was 18 inches in diameter. The pump was 6 inches and steam cylinder 10½ inches with 14 inch stroke, yoke motion. The valves of pump were hinge pattern and made of brass. The receiving screw and vacuum chamber were located at the bottom of the pump. The air chamber and discharge gates were on

VIGILANT ENGINE, PHILADELPHIA.

Built by Hunnsworth, Eakin & Co. Same pattern as Reanie & Neafie.

the top. While working, she remained quite still, with the exception of that vibratory motion which is peculiar to all horizontal machines.

In the latter part of August, 1858, this engine was sent to Boston, Mass., to take part in the grand steam fire-engine contest. The trial took place on "Boston Common" Aug. 31st and Sept. 1st. The engines competing were four in number and built by the following firms: G. M. Bird & Co. of East Boston, Bean & Scott of Lawrence, Mass., Hinckley & Drury, Boston, and Reanie & Neafie of Philadelphia. The trial of the first day commenced at about 9 A. M., and as the Philadelphian drew the A, she was first to commence. The first test was to fill a tank holding 2,500 gallons. It was accomplished in 11 minutes 8 seconds. It took 8 minutes 28 seconds to raise 60 lbs. of steam. At the horizontal play, which was through 200 feet of 3 inch hose with a $1\frac{1}{4}$ inch nozzle, she played 163 feet. In the perpendicular play, she attained the height of 110 feet.

After each engine had played according to the rules governing the tests, each was allowed to play as they chose. The "Philadelphia" played at the flag-staff with their large rubber hose and threw a stream 150 feet high. Tremont hand-engine, No. 12, of the Boston department, was in attendance to pump boiler water for the steamers, and when the contest was over, they played a stream at the staff and forced it fully and fairly over the top, beating all the steamers.

The following day, Wednesday, Sept. 1st, the trial of speed came off ; which was a run around the Common, a distance of $1\frac{1}{4}$ miles, reel off 200 feet of hose, and get water through a pipe ; the engines to start with cold water. This was considered a part of the trial for prizes offered by programme ; each to start at intervals of 5 minutes and each to fire up at a given point on Beacon Street. The "Philadelphia" started at just 6 minutes 20 seconds past 11, and came down Beacon Street on the run, arriving at the firing point at 15 minutes past 11, and got water at 27 minutes 26 seconds past 11. A few minutes after, they had four streams on. The "Philadelphia" was awarded the first prize of $500.

On their way home, they stopped in New York City, and much censure was cast upon a few members of the New York department. It seems the committee arrived in that city in advance of their engine ; and on the day previous to the arrival of their engine, visited Mayor Tiemann and obtained permission to exhibit the engine in the Park. On the morning that the trial was to take place, a fire broke out in the city and several of the Philadelphia firemen were present. Hearing that their engine had arrived from Boston, they left the fire to take charge of her and get her ready for the trial which was to take place at 9 A. M. After they had got her to the Park, the Mayor, at some one's suggestion, desired that they might try her on the fire, which, at that time, was slowly burning, but confined to the building. The New York companies having been discharged, with three or four exceptions, the men with the steamer were in doubt whether to take the offer ; when Engineer Cornwell arrived in the Park and offered to give them a chance to play upon the ruins of the fire, promising to obtain a supply of water for them. Having confidence in the engineer, they started forthwith ; and, much to their chagrin, were hailed on their arrival with jeers and shouts of derision. Their intention was to retire immediately to the Park, as their reception at the fire was anything but satisfactory. But, as the engineer had invited them there, they considered themselves under his protection, and had nerve enough to stand and play, notwithstanding the whole rabble, firemen and all, were working against them and deriding their efforts to get near the fire. Engine No. 6, to their credit be it spoken, gave them their hydrant, and with all the opposition against them, they succeeded in throwing a fine stream.

Their playing was not as effective as it might have been for the reason, that, while they were shifting about in search of water, the steam rose to such a pressure that it was necessary to haul out the fire from under the boiler. The steamer was also short of hose and was compelled to stand to windward of the fire, the wind, of course, blowing the spray of their steamer, which went on the men working on Engine No. 31, which company were playing against them, and wet, as the foreman of 31 said, very nearly everybody

GOOD INTENT NO. 30, PHILADELPHIA.
Built by S. W. Landell & Co.

about the fire. The men at the pipe, after getting wet, which was no fault of the men in charge of the steam engine, deliberately turned their pipe on the Philadelphians, wetting them but slightly, they being almost out of range of their water. At this moment some persons made a rush at some of the strangers. They were firemen, some with caps and some with badges. But their intentions, whatever they were, were cut short by one of the engineers requesting that the steam-engine be taken away, which was accordingly done.

The Philadelphia hose members immediately started for the Park, where they commenced preparation for another trial, but a despatch being sent for them to come home, as an escort would be waiting for them, they departed without any further playing. It might be expected that they went home impressed with anything but a sense of the kindly feeling which had heretofore existed between the Philadelphia and New York firemen. But no! they very properly kept their own counsel, and had it not been for the accounts given through the public press, but few out of New York would have known of the affair.

Shortly after, a meeting of the board of engineers was held in New York City, pursuant to a call signed by a number of the officers of the department for the purpose of taking steps relative to the alleged insult offered to the Philadelphia Hose Company during their visit to that city. The meeting was called to order by the chief engineer who stated the object of the meeting, and Mr. Robert Rogers, of Engine Company 14, offered the following resolutions : —

" *Whereas*, The public press of New York and Philadelphia have censured the New York fire department for the act of discourtesy shown towards the Philadelphia Hose Company No. 1 on their recent visit to this city when returning home from a successful competition with the steam fire-engines of Boston, and,

" *Whereas*, This board do not consider that the fire department of the city of New York should be held accountable for the acts of a few of its members, be it therefore,

" *Resolved*, That we disclaim any act of incivility shown towards our friends of Philadelphia, knowing them to be gentlemen whose hospitality towards New York firemen visiting their city is proverbial, and a company whose acts have done more to perpetuate a good volunteer system for extinguishing fires than any other in the state.

" *Resolved*, That we heartily regret that the Philadelphia Hose Company should have left our city with feelings other than of good-will, caused by the reception given them while at the fire in the ' Bowery,' they having come upon the grounds at the invitation of His Honor, the Mayor, and one of the engineers of the department, and can only account for the disrespect shown, from a combination of circumstances producing a feeling against steam apparatus, and not from any intentional discourtesy towards the gentlemen composing the committee in charge of the steam engine.

" *Resolved*, That the officers of this board be directed to transmit a copy of these resolutions to the President of the Philadelphia Hose Company."

On arrival home, a grand reception was given them by several companies in the Quaker City, and by the workmen employed by Reanie & Neafie to the number of two hundred. The procession numbered over 1,000 men, and a great variety of transparencies bearing exultant mottoes were displayed. The Philadelphia Hose-house was splendidly illuminated and decorated with flags and mottoes; and when the procession arrived there, the enthusiasm of the crowd broke forth in tremendous cheers and shouts of victory. Happily, it passed off without any fights or firemen's riots, for which Philadelphia, at that time, was famous.

All of the Reanie & Neafie engines had square grates. The first Class was 30 inches square; second Class, 28 inches square; third Class, 22 inches square. The first-class engine weighed about 9,000 lbs., pump 6 inches, steam cylinder 12 inches and 14-inch stroke. The second-class engine weighed about 6,000 lbs., pump $4\frac{1}{2}$ inches, steam-cylinder 8 inches and 12-inch stroke. The third-class engine weighed about 5,000 lbs., pump 4 inches, steam-cylinder 7 inches, and 10-inch stroke. The engine built for the Hibernia Company was extra large, having a $6\frac{1}{2}$ inch pump, $11\frac{1}{2}$ inch steam-cylinder, and 14 inch stroke. Several of their engines were built with 16 inch stroke. Most of

BUILT BY THE PHILADELPHIA HYDRAULIC WORKS.

the machines built by this company were what were termed Cylindrical-Frame engines; but they built several that were known as slab-frame. On these engines the front wheels turned under the same as on a crane-neck engine. The following are a few of the places that used this noted build of engine. The second was a duplicate of the first, was named "Alpha" and sold to Baltimore, Md. The eleventh, the "Gen. Clinch," went to Augusta, Ga. The thirteenth, "Pioneer," was sold to Providence, R. I. The fourteenth was built for Madison, Ind. The seventeenth was the "Gen. Meigs" and went to Washington, D. C. The eighteenth went to Nashville, Tenn. The twentieth was sold to St. Louis, Mo. The twenty-first went to New Orleans, La. The twenty-second was named " Pennsylvania " and was sold to San Francisco, Cal.   The twenty-third was built for Mobile, Ala.   The twenty-fifth was named " Gen. Butler," and sold to Norfolk, Va. The thirty-eighth went to La Atravida, Cuba.

So it can be easily seen that this engine found a ready market in all parts of the country.   The third engine built by this firm, the " Hope " hose engine, is still in existence ; and was owned and cherished for several years by the late Thomas Peto of Philadelphia, who was, at one time, a member of that company.   A short time ago, he presented this engine, on conditions, to Riverside Fire Company No. 1 of Riverside, N. J.

Reanie & Neafie discontinued building steam fire-engines in about the year 1870. Mr. Parry claimed to have been the first to apply a churn or circulating valve to the pumps of an engine.   He was an engineer in the navy during the war of the rebellion.

Mr. Parry also built, on the same general plan, four engines at the shops of S. W. Landell & Co.   The engines built by Hunnsworth, Eakin & Co. were also of the same style and had the Parry pump.   His last engine was built at the Philadelphia Hydraulic Works.

E. V. MERRICK & SON—1858.

E. V. Merrick of Philadelphia built, as near as can be ascertained, three steam Fire-Engines; the first two of which were turned out in 1858, and had what was known as "Coney" pumps. The first one had twelve, six on either side, which were single acting and operated by a vertical disk between them. The second had ten pumps, five on either side; while the third or last, which was built in 1859 for the Weccacoe Engine Company No. 19 of the Volunteer Fire Department of the city of Philadelphia, differed entirely from the others, having two reciprocating pumps which were placed horizontally at the

WECCACOE ENGINE NO. 19, PHILADELPHIA
Built by E. V. Merrick.

forward part of the engine directly over the forward axle and measured 6 inches in diameter by 15-inch stroke. The steam-cylinders were placed horizontally at the side of the boiler and measured $8\frac{1}{2}$ inches in diameter with 15-inch stroke and were worked by a crank motion. This machine cost $3,500 and was used but a very short time. At the Fair of the Pennsylvania State Agricultural Society, held at West Philadelphia Sept. 28, 29, 30, 1859, it competed against seven other steamers, retiring with eighth place, playing only 109 feet horizontally, through 200 feet of hose. This engine is still in existence at the League Island Navy Yard, where the rust is getting in its fine work to perfection.

G. M. BIRD & CO.—1858.

The firm of G. M. Bird & Co., of East Boston, is one of the many that tried their skill at building Steam Fire-Engines; and, like several others, their first engine proved to be their last.

This machine was built in 1858. Her length was 13 feet 10 inches, width 6 feet, height 11 feet, weight about 9,000 lbs. She was placed on four wheels, which were $4\frac{1}{2}$ feet in diameter behind, and $2\frac{1}{2}$ feet forward. She rested on rubber springs with steel bands; and could be drawn by two horses with ease. The pump and steam cylinder were single, and lay horizontally with the frame. Her pump was $6\frac{1}{2}$ inches in diameter, steam-cylinder 10 inches in diameter with 14-inch stroke. The inlets were on either side and she could also take water from a large tank that was attached to the engine, measuring $4\frac{1}{2}$ feet in length, 20 inches depth, holding 150 gallons; thereby, making her capable of taking water from hydrants or hand-engines. Her boiler was tubular, 3 feet 6 inches in diameter, having 180 iron smoke tubes 4 feet in length by 2 inches in breadth, and contained 375 feet of fire surface. This boiler could make steam in about eight minutes. The suction hose was $4\frac{1}{2}$ inches in diameter. There were four outlets, which were calculated to be able to supply four hand-engines or throw four good fire streams. The pump, water ways and all parts of the engine that were liable to come in contact with salt water, were made of brass or copper. The works of this engine were so arranged that every part was within easy reach of the engineer.

On June 25th, 1858, at 5.15 P. M., this machine was fired up for the first time, and in eight minutes steam was on; but she was not immediately put to work. About two hours were occupied by a series of experiments, which were rendered somewhat unsatisfactory by the continual bursting of hose. Mr. Bird did not intend this to be a public trial, as the engine was not wholly finished; and she was only tried to see if any improvements could be made before completing her. However, quite a large number of spectators were present.

The next test that this engine received was at the great trial of steam fire-engines on Boston Common, Aug. 31st and Sept. 1st, 1858. The rules for the first day were to fill a tank holding 2,500 gallons, and time to be taken on raising 60 lbs. of steam; distance playing, both horizontal and perpendicular, through 200 feet of 3-inch hose. The time occupied in filling the tank was 8 minutes 25 seconds. Sixty lbs. of steam was raised in 13 minutes 51 seconds. The horizontal stream was thrown 140 feet, the perpendicular stream 130 feet.

The second day was a trial of speed, which was to run around the Common, a distance of $1\frac{1}{4}$ miles, lay 200 feet of hose and get water through the same ; all engines to start with cold water in the boilers. This was considered part of the trial for prizes offered by programme, each to start at intervals of 5 minutes, and each engine to commence firing up at a given point on Beacon Street. This engine was the second to make the run and started at 11 minutes 39 seconds past 11, reached the firing up point at 25 minutes $30\frac{1}{2}$ seconds past 11, and arrived at the pond 29 minutes 43 seconds past 11 ; commenced to play at 38 minutes 25 seconds past 11. At times, when the steam was up to 120 lbs., she threw a vertical stream to the height of about 175 feet through a $1\frac{1}{4}$-inch nozzle.

The prizes were awarded as follows : Reanie & Neafie, Philadelphia builders, first prize, $500 ; Bean & Scott of Lawrence, second prize, $300 ; G. M. Bird & Co., East Boston, third prize, $200 ; and the fourth engine competing, built by Hinckley & Drury of Boston, "got left."

On the third of December, this engine was again tested, taking water from a hydrant, and commenced playing with 60 lbs. of steam, which was made in 8 minutes from the time of lighting the fire. She played through 100 feet of hose, using a $1\frac{1}{4}$-inch nozzle, and sent a horizontal stream 201 feet, and two streams through 1-inch nozzles to the distance of 176 feet each. At the end of the trial, the steam had increased to 120 lbs. and was blowing off.

This engine was never sold or used for fire purposes, and was shortly after broken up.

MURRAY & HAZLEHURST — 1858.

The firm of Murray & Hazlehurst of Baltimore, Md., go on record as having built five or six Steam Fire-Engines. Their first was built in 1858 for the Washington Engine Company No. 13 of the Volunteer Fire Dept. of that city. Subsequently, they received

BUILT BY MURRAY & HAZLEHURST.

an order from the city for three more. It is believed that these machines did not meet with very good success and but very little is known of them. Worthington, of New York City, designed and built the steam pumps for all of them, which measured 5 inches in diameter. The reader will have to draw an idea of this build of engine from the engraving, which is a fine representation of their last one, built in 1860, which was named "Thom's King" and was shipped to Savannah, Ga., in that year.

BEAN & SCOTT — 1858.

Bean & Scott built their first, last and only steam fire-engine in Lawrence, Mass., in the year 1858. The boiler of this engine was 29½ inches in diameter, of the common tubular style, placed vertically at the rear of the machine, and contained 199 1½ inch welded iron smoke tubes 30 inches in length. Her machinery was nowhere in sight, as it was encased with wood, which covered the working parts completely up, except the balance-wheels. It had a running board, similar to a locomotive, that went from the boiler straight around the frame, for the engineer to walk on. The pump and steam-cylinder were placed horizontally. The pump was 6 inches in diameter, steam cylinder 9 inches in diameter, with a 14-inch stroke. The length of engine was 14 feet, height 8 feet 6 inches, width 7 feet. The frame was straight, and the forward wheels were low, so that they could turn under. The inlets were on either side. The air-chamber was very large and of acorn shape. There was also a large feed water tank on the forward part of the engine, on top of which was the driver's seat. The total weight was about four tons. This engine was first tested June 28, 1858. She was brought upon the trial grounds at 9 A. M., when a fire of shavings and light pine wood was lighted under her. In 11½ minutes the pump was started, and with a steam pressure of 60 lbs., the machine commenced playing through three lines of hose, each 25 feet in length and pipes with 1 inch nozzles. The result was that the three streams, playing perpendicularly, reached a height of between 135 and 140 feet. At 23 minutes after 9, the pressure of steam had increased to 70 lbs. and the pump pressure 55 lbs., when a fourth stream was put on. In five minutes, the pressure of steam had increased to 120 lbs., with the furnace door open and steam escaping quite freely from the safety valve. The four streams reached a per-pendicular height of 137 feet. She then threw two streams horizontally 152 feet each, and the other two streams 162 feet each.

The second trial was with two lines of hose, each 50 feet in length with pipes and nozzles 1¼ inches. The playing commenced at 40 minutes past 9, with 121 lbs. of steam, and a pump pressure of 70 lbs. At 9.45, the machine working with 90 lbs. pump pressure and making 200 revolutions per minute, one of the streams got away from the pipemen in charge of it. Then the hose crooked up like a serpent and burst, upsetting several of the spectators. The result of this playing was not ascertained, owing to this accident. At 9.58, the machine commenced playing with 120 lbs. steam pressure and 85 lbs. water, with two lengths of hose. One went 130 feet with 1-inch nozzle, and the other 125 feet with 1¼-inch nozzle. In one minute and a half, the pump pressure increased to 130 lbs.; the engine now making 240 revolutions per minute, with fire-door open and steam blowing off freely, when the hose burst. The result of this trial was that both streams threw horizontally 192 feet 6 inches. At the third trial, while the engine was working under a steam pressure of 120 lbs. and a water pressure of 95 lbs., the hose again burst, and no result was taken. At the fourth and last trial, with 120 lbs. steam pressure and 145 lbs. water pressure, the engine, playing through 135 feet of hose and using a 1½ inch nozzle, sent a horizontal stream 198 feet. The engine worked with great ease and the engineers and other prominent men present were greatly pleased. At a trial a few days later, this engine filled a tank holding 1,600 gallons, playing through one line of hose, in 3¼ minutes, and with four lines of hose in 2½ minutes.

LAWRENCE NO. 7.

Built by Bean & Scott.

The next test that this engine received was at the great trial of engines on Boston Common on Aug. 31st and Sept. 1st, 1858. There were four competitors; a Reanie & Neafie of Philadelphia; an engine built by Hinckley and Drury of Boston; another built by G. M. Bird of East Boston and the Bean & Scott of Lawrence. On the first day, Aug. 31st, the test was to fill a tank holding 2,500 gallons, and time to be taken in raising 60 lbs. of steam, and distance playing to be horizontal and vertical through 200 feet of 3 inch hose. Sixty pounds of steam was raised in 14 minutes 10 seconds. There was some little difficulty experienced, but from what cause, I am unable to learn. After having played some five minutes, they withdrew, on account of a desire on their part not to keep their water up to the first gage-cock. The committee thinking the danger was great when there was no possible means of knowing where the water in the boiler was (a very just conclusion, of course), she withdrew. The second day of the trial, Sept. 1st, the Lawrence engine was again on the grounds. The tests this day were to be a trial of speed which was to be a run around the Common, a distance of $1\frac{1}{4}$ miles; to reel off 200 feet of hose and get water through the pipe; the engines to start with cold water. This was considered a part of the trial for prizes offered by programme; each to start at intervals of five minutes, and each engine to fire up at a given point on Beacon Street. The Bean & Scott was the third to give the exhibition and started at 15 minutes 23 seconds past 11 and commenced firing up at 29 minutes 11 seconds past 11, arriving at the pond at 32 minutes $47\frac{1}{2}$ seconds past 11; commenced playing at 46 minutes 58 seconds past 11 through a 1 inch nozzle to the height of about 175 feet. She then played open butt to the distance of about 65 feet. The next exhibition she gave was through two lines with 1 inch nozzles, throwing vertically; and succeeded in completely wetting the flag at the top of the staff, a distance of about 155 feet, using 130 lbs. of steam and 150 lbs. water pressure, and kept the water of both streams at that point for over ten minutes.

The second prize of $300 was awarded to this engine, the first of $500 being won by the Philadelphia engine. This machine was sold to the City of Boston for $3,500, and was named " Lawrence No. 7." She was in active service until 1862, when she was discarded. She was afterwards sold to the Norway Iron Works, at South Boston, and was used for some time for pumping purposes; but was finally broken up. Mr. N. S. Bean afterwards went to Manchester, N. H., and there superintended the building of the Amoskeag engines. Mr. Scott still resides in Lawrence, Mass.

POOLE & HUNT — 1858.

Foremost among the Maryland builds of Steam Fire Engines were those constructed by Poole & Hunt of Baltimore, which firm completed their first steamer in 1858, continuing in business until 1868. During the ten years engaged in this work, they built fourteen engines in various sizes, all being of the horizontal pattern. The steam-cylinders were single, varying in size from 9 to $14\frac{1}{2}$ inches in diameter. The pumps, which were

WASHINGTON NO. 14, PHILADELPHIA.
Built by Poole & Hunt.

of the "Fulton" pattern, were double acting, consisting of two horizontal barrels, one over the other, each containing two pistons on one piston-rod, the pistons being fitted with rubber valves on them. The two pump-rods were attached to a crosshead which was attached to the steam piston-rod; so that one steam-cylinder and piston-rod worked both pump-rods and four pistons simultaneously in either direction with a direct horizontal movement, being steadied by a connecting rod which was attached to the crosshead and balance-wheel. The boiler used on these engines was upright, multi-tubular, with square fire-box and enlarged steam space.

The second class engine boilers having $239\frac{1}{2}$ square feet of heating surface could raise sufficient steam to start the engine from cold water in from five to seven minutes from time of lighting the fire. The weight of these machines varied from 5,000 to 9,000 lbs. The following are the dimensions of their second class engines: one steam cylinder 11 inches in diameter, with 12 inch stroke of piston, one double pump, double acting, each

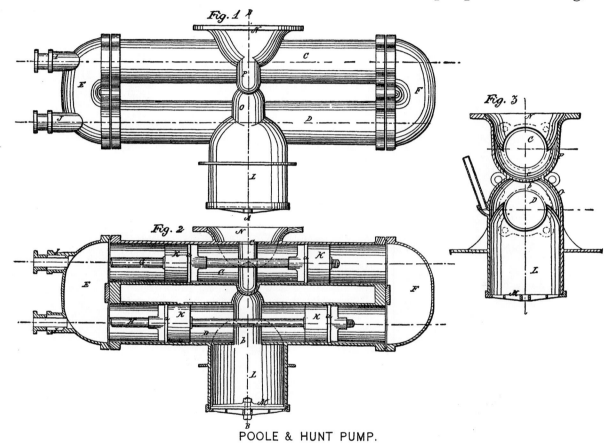

POOLE & HUNT PUMP.

barrel of which measured $4\frac{1}{2}$ inches in diameter with 12 inch stroke. The inlet, which was at the forward end of the pump, was $4\frac{1}{2}$ inches in diameter. The outlets were $2\frac{1}{2}$ inches in diameter.

One of these largest sizes was built for the Washington Engine Company No. 14 of the Volunteer Fire Department of the city of Philadelphia in 1858 and was in continual use in the heart of that city for over 30 years; but was finally disposed of on account of it being antique and rather heavy; otherwise, it was still in fair condition and capable of coping with the fiery element for years to come, which speaks well for the principle of its construction and the workmanship of these machines.

HINCKLEY & DRURY — 1858.

Hinckley & Drury built their first Steam Fire-Engine at the "Boston Locomotive Works" in 1858. This engine was named the "New Era," and was designed by Mr. J. M. Stone.

The boiler was of the common tubular pattern, measuring 36 inches in diameter, with

MAZEPPA NO. I, BOSTON, MASS.
Built by Hinckley & Drury.

241 smoke tubes $1\frac{1}{2}$ inches in diameter and 4 feet in length, which were made of brass. The frame was slightly craned so as to allow the front wheels to turn under. The pump and steam cylinder were placed horizontally and were single. The pump was double acting, 7 inches in diameter, with 12 inch stroke; steam cylinder 12 inches in diameter, 12 inch stroke. The weight was about 10,000 lbs.

The "New Era" took part in the famous trial of steam fire-engines on Boston Common on Aug. 31st and Sept. 1st, 1858, against three other builds, but was defeated by each of the competitors. On Dec. 4th, same year, she was again tried at the "South

End," Boston, against the "Eclipse," an engine built for Boston by Silsby, Mynderse & Co. of Seneca Falls, N. Y. They drew water from the south bay 17 feet lift. At precisely 2.56 P. M. both fired up and at 3.04, the "Eclipse" commenced playing with 10 lbs. of steam. With 63 lbs., it played horizontally through 100 feet of hose, with 1¼ inch nozzle, a distance of 161 feet; with 1½ inch nozzle, 144 feet; and vertically, through same nozzle, 140 feet. It also played vertically through 1⅛ inch and 1¼ inch nozzle, 150 feet. The "New Era" at 3.15 had 80 lbs. of steam and played one horizontal stream through 1¼ inch nozzle, 100 feet. At 3.19, the gauge denoted 88 lbs. It played at its highest pressure through 1¼ inch nozzle 165 feet and through 1½ inch nozzle 144 feet horizontally, and through same nozzle, vertically, 140 feet. Another trial was to be had, drawing water from a hydrant; but the great weight of the "New Era" sunk it into the loose dirt at the wharf and it could not take part in this trial. This machine was never sold and was shortly after broken up.

Mr. Stone had probably heard the old adage, "If at first you don't succeed, try, try again." In the year 1859, another engine was built from his design, which proved to be a powerful machine. It had a large waste boiler, to which was attached a long, cylindrical tank which formed the frame on which was placed the pump and steam cylinder, which were single and horizontal. The pump and steam cylinder were placed close together; the pump at the forward part of the engine, the piston rod passing through both, and was worked at the rear of the steam cylinder by a link motion with balance wheel. The inlet was forward at the base of the pump. The air-chamber was very large, cylindrical shaped, with fancy brass top, and signal light above. The discharge gates were at the base of the air-chamber. The pump was 5 inches in diameter, 13 inch stroke, steam cylinder 8½ inches in diameter. She was hung on platform springs forward and spiral behind. The total weight was 10,500 lbs. This engine was sold to the city of Boston for $2,500; less than half what it cost to build her. She was named "Rob Roy," but better known as "Mazeppa" No. 1. This engine was kept in active service until 1872, when it was discarded on account of its great weight and shortly afterwards went into the junk heap. This was the last engine built by the "Boston Locomotive Works."

AMOSKEAG — 1859.

The Amoskeag Steam Fire Engines were built by the Amoskeag Manufacturing Company of Manchester, N. H. They need no praise from my pen, as their far famed

EAGLE NO. 3, BOSTON, MASS.
Rotary Pump Engine Built by the Amoskeag Manufacturing Co.

reputation is only too well known, not only from ocean to ocean on this continent, but in the far distant lands of Asia.

Their first engine was built in 1859, was of the mongrel type, designed by Mr. N. S. Bean and was tested on July 4th; raising steam and playing two streams to the height of 203 feet in seven minutes from time of lighting fire. The boiler was vertical and tubular with square fire-box and contracted waist. The frame which was cylindrical in form and 18 inches in diameter, served as a feed-water tank and contained the air-chamber and delivery pipes. The steam-cylinders were double and were attached to the boiler in a vertical position, measuring $7\frac{3}{4}$ inches in diameter with 12 inch stroke. Directly under the frame or water tank and next to the boiler was a rotary pump of the

ARBA READ NO. I, TROY, NEW YORK.

Single Pump Barrel Tank Engine, Built by the Amoskeag Manufacturing Co.

"Amoskeag" pattern, to the shaft of which were attached two solid steel balance-wheels, one on either side; and connecting rods from these wheels to the sliding-blocks gave the pump its power. The inlets were on either side of the pump. The outlets were four in number and located at the forward end of the feed-water tank. The height of boiler to the top of smoke-stack was 11 feet, length of engine 11 feet, width $5\frac{1}{2}$ feet, weight 5,500 lbs. without fuel or water.

This engine was named "Amoskeag, No. 1" and sold to the City of Manchester for

SINGLE PUMP U TANK ENGINE.

Built by the Amoskeag Manufacturing Co.

the sum of $3,000, where it was in constant service for seventeen years. Only eleven of these rotary engines were built.

This firm constructed several styles of engines from time to time which I will endeavor to partially describe in their order. The second style was built in 1860, and was similar in appearance to the others, with the exception of the pumps, which were double acting and of the plunger style (having 8 poppett valves on each head), and made in two sizes. The same year, they built another design, called the "U" tank; so named on account of the water-tank which formed the frame being formed in the shape

SINGLE PUMP HARP FRAME ENGINE.
Built by the Amoskeag Manufacturing Co.

of the letter U. These engines were built in one size and were single, having only one double acting pump and one steam-cylinder. The weight was 5,000 lbs., and they could with ease be drawn by hand.

In 1861, they produced another style, known as the "Harp" engine. The frame was cast in brass, hexagon in shape, and was bolted to the pump and steam-cylinder, giving it the resemblance to the frame of a harp. These engines were built in three sizes, the smallest, or third size, being very light, weighing only 4,000 lbs. The pumps were double acting. The first size measured 6 inches in diameter with 12-inch stroke. In 1862, they built for the city of Troy, N. Y., a barrel or cylindrical frame engine, similar to the large double machines, only it had but one pump and steam-cylinder which measured 6 by 12 inches. But three of these engines were built.

In 1866, their first double straight frame engine was built and sold to the city of New York. This engine was rated as second size and weighed about 6,000 lbs. The pumps were 4⅛ inches in diameter by 8-inch stroke, steam cylinder 6⅞ inches diameter by 8-inch stroke. These engines, at that time, were considered as good as any in the market.

In the year 1870 a great improvement was made by building them crane-neck, as they could be turned around in a much smaller space than the straight frames. These engines were double and built in two sizes, the largest of which weighed about 7,500 lbs., pumps 4½ inches in diameter, 8-inch stroke, steam-cylinder 7⅝ inches in diameter, 8-inch stroke. The second size weighed about 6,500 lbs., pumps 4¼ inches in diameter, 8-inch stroke, steam-cylinder 6⅞ inches in diameter, 8-inch stroke. The boilers were upright and tubular in style, containing about 300 brass smoke-tubes 18 inches long and 1¼ inches in diameter. These boilers were very simple in construction, and for safety, strength and durability were unsurpassed. The connections to the steam-cylinder were entirely unexposed, which was a great advantage. The pumps were double acting and placed vertically, and for effectiveness, reliability and durability were unsurpassed by any other plunger pump. It was arranged for receiving the suction-hose on either side unless otherwise ordered. The delivery-pipes were at the base of the air-chamber, and two in number. The material used in the construction of these engines, and their workmanship were of the best quality and were fully guaranteed. Several of these engines were sold in the South and were models of beauty.

In 1877, they constructed a very light engine, suitable for small towns and villages. They were what is styled a "Single Short Frame," fourth size machine, weighing only 3,800 lbs. The pump was 4¼ inches in diameter, 8-inch stroke, steam-cylinder 6⅞ inches in diameter, 8-inch stroke.

In the year 1872, they commenced building self-propelling engines, but they were not generally approved of, although, in some places, they were used with success. The heaviest and most powerful of these machines was built for the city of Hartford, Conn., in 1889 and is in service at the present time. It is the largest steam fire-engine in the world. The height to the top of the smoke-stack is 9 feet 9 inches, length of engine 15 feet. The boiler is vertical, 40 inches in diameter, and contains 301 copper tubes. The pumps are double and measure 5½ inches in diameter with 8 inch stroke. The steam-cylinders are 9½ inches in diameter by 8-inch stroke. It is arranged with rod and cross-head connections between the steam-cylinders and pumps, which is made necessary by its propelling features; so that the motion of the engine can be changed or reversed. The method of self-propelling is secured by means of a continuation of the main crank-shaft working with suitable gears upon a compound shaft, upon each end of which there are wheels connecting with the two driving-wheels by endless chains. Upon this shaft is arranged a compound or equalizer which permits the engine to turn corners without loss of power. The surroundings of the engineer's place are very convenient, being similar to those on an ordinary locomotive, with throttle, reversing lever, etc., close at hand. The

DOUBLE STRAIGHT FRAME ENGINE.
Built by the Amoskeag Manufacturing Co.

FIRST SIZE DOUBLE ENGINE.

Built by the Manchester Locomotive Works.

steering is performed by the action of a pair of gears and a worm-gear connected with the forward axle ; the whole being under the direct control of the steersman, who occupies the driver's seat. On a fair road, this engine can make over 10 miles an hour, and for winter service spike-tires are provided. It contains many other advantages which can only be brought out by a drawing and a technical description. It has about double the capacity of an ordinary engine for throwing water, and, as compared in size, looms up proportionally. The suction-hose is 6 inches in diameter, and the discharge-gates $3\frac{1}{2}$ inches in diameter. The hind-wheels are 5 feet in height with 4 inch spokes, and 4 inch tire with $3\frac{3}{4}$ inch axle. Each rear-wheel weighs 1085 lbs. while the engine, in its entirety, weighs something over 8 tons. It is handsomely nickel plated and painted, presenting a very natty appearance. A pole can be attached, which makes it optional whether horses or steam shall be used as a motive power.

A short time ago, this firm constructed an engine, named the " Abe Lincoln," which was worked by a crank motion without link-blocks ; but as no committees have, as yet, fallen in love with it, it still remains in the factory.

Over 700 engines have been sold from their establishment. In the spring of 1877, a change in the management was made and the " Manchester Locomotive Works " became the owners and are still conducting the business.

The best results ever attained from one of these engines were at the trial test of a first-size machine built for the city of Cambridge, Mass., and known as " Big 6." She is a large, powerful machine hung on " Endicott's Patent Platform Springs," and with all the latest improvements, weighing 9,500 lbs. with water and fuel. The steam-cylinders are $7\frac{5}{8}$ inches in diameter, 8-inch stroke, pumps $4\frac{5}{8}$ inches in diameter, 8-inch stroke, with a capacity of 900 gallons per minute. The boiler is steel and contains 241 copper smoke tubes $1\frac{1}{2}$ inches in diameter, 24 inches long. This machine received her delivery test on Mar. 14, 1891, drafting her water from Fresh Pond. Thirty lbs. of steam were raised from cold water in six minutes from time of lighting fire, when the engine was put in motion and in 45 seconds after, the stream had reached the distance of 100 feet. At the expiration of 9 minutes from the time of firing up, the steam-gauge indicated 100 lbs. and the stream reached the distance of 321 feet. This play was made through 100 feet of hose, simesed, using a $1\frac{1}{4}$ inch nozzle. The next test was through the same amount of hose with a $1\frac{3}{8}$ inch nozzle, and a steam pressure of 140 lbs. and water pressure of 250 lbs.; when a magnificent stream of water was thrown horizontally to the distance of 381 feet $4\frac{1}{2}$ inches. Two streams were then thrown simultaneously with $1\frac{1}{2}$ and $1\frac{5}{8}$ inch nozzle with splendid results.

In 1892, this firm constructed an extra large engine which is rated as " Extra First Size," the first two of which were built for the city of Detroit, Mich. These machines are very powerful when at a draft or whenever there is a sufficient supply of water to be obtained. The following are the dimensions. Height over all 10 feet. Length over all 24 feet 9 inches. Width over all (ordinary) 6 feet 5 inches. Weight without supplies

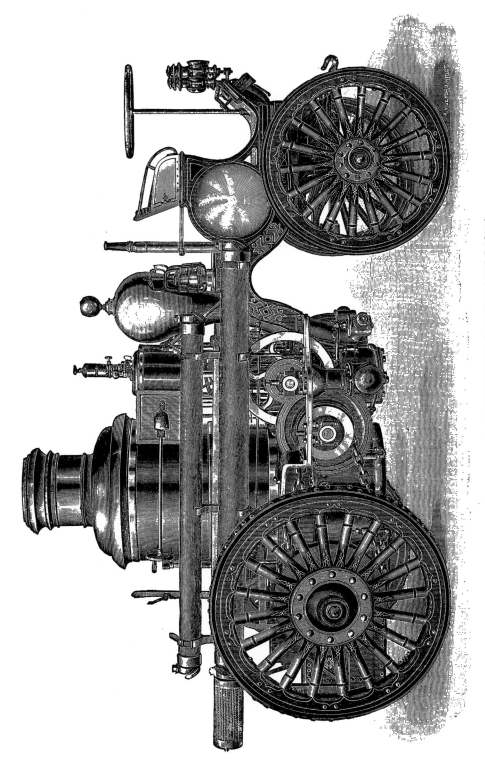

HARTFORD, CONN., SELF-PROPELLING STEAM FIRE-ENGINE.

Built by the Manchester Locomotive Works.

FOURTH SIZE SINGLE SHORT FRAME ENGINE.
Built by the Manchester Locomotive Works.

about 9,000 lbs.   Pumps 5 inches in diameter, 8-inch stroke.   Steam cylinders 8½ inches in diameter, 8-inch stroke.   These machines are guaranteed to deliver 1,100 gallons per minute.   The following letter from the Fire Commission of Detroit gives a most remarkable account of a capacity test of these two engines.

FIRE COMMISSION OF DETROIT, MICHIGAN.

Office of the Secretary,

DETROIT, MICH., December 28, 1892.

A. Blood, Esq., Agent Manchester Locomotive Works, Manchester, N. H.:

DEAR SIR : — Enclosed please find draft No. 295,505 on the National Bank of Commerce of New York for the sum of ———— in payment of Engines Nos. 686 and 687, as per your invoice of Dec. 1, 1892.   Kindly forward your receipt for the same to this office.

These engines were tested by the Fire Commission one week ago to-day, and with the most satisfactory results.   The engines were operated by Engineer Cornelius Bresnahan of Engine Company No. 3, under the supervision of Francis Beaufait, Master Mechanic of this department; and I beg to assure you that had these gentlemen been the personal representatives of the Manchester Locomotive Works, your interests would not have been in better hands.   Both of these gentlemen have operated Amoskeag engines for more than a generation and regard them as the " Ne Plus Ultra " of fire extinguishing apparatus.

The tests for capacity were made by pumping direct from a tank capable of holding 2,250 gallons.   No. 3, running at her greatest speed, pumped 1,875 gallons in fifty seconds by stop watch.   No. 1, running at the speed which would be given her in ordinary fire service, pumped the same quantity of water in fifty-seven seconds.   Using No. 3 for distance throwing, she astonished all beholders by throwing a solid stream, 1⅝ inches in diameter, three hundred feet, while No. 1 delivered two solid 1½ inch streams, the like of which was never seen before by any one connected with this department.

I might multiply words expressing to you the sentiments of the Commissioners and Officers of the Detroit Fire Department as to these engines.   They are certainly noble specimens of mechanism.   They do credit to the institution which put them forth, and they will do as much to perpetuate the reputation of the old Amoskeag as any machine your company has ever turned out.   Our only regret is that we are not able at this time to place an order with you for two more.   Yours truly,

(Signed)   JAMES E. TRYON, Secretary.

JAMES NELSON — 1859.

In 1859, James Nelson of Pittsburgh, Pa., designed a Steam Fire-Engine for the Eagle Steam Fire Engine Company No. 1, of that city, which was built by the members of that company under the supervision of Mr. George Wilson of that city, who devoted

EAGLE S. F. E. NO. I, PITTSBURGH, PA.
Designed by James Nelson.

the whole of his time until completed, being assisted, at times, by several members of the company who were machinists putting in their spare time and evenings.

This machine was constructed with a straight frame, cylindrical in form, upon which were placed, in a horizontal position, two steam cylinders, both being cast in one piece, and measuring $6\frac{1}{4}$ inches in diameter. Forward of the steam cylinders and in line with them, were placed two pumps which were also cast in one piece, being double acting, measuring 4 inches in diameter with 12-inch stroke of piston. The boiler, which was placed vertically, was very long and of a peculiar design, being made in two sections, the lower section of which contained the smoke tubes, which were 17 inches in length. Around the upper part of this half was a brass ring, on top of which was placed the top

(63)

half of the boiler, which also had a corresponding ring. The face of these rings was tongued and grooved and ground steam tight and bolted firmly together. Through these rings was bored a series of $\frac{1}{2}$ inch holes, which allowed of the steam passing from the bottom section into the top half which served as a reservoir or steam-dome. The fire, after passing through the smoke-flues of the lower half, came in contact with the inner sheet of the top section, which was cone-shaped, thereby super-heating the steam. The feed water passed through a heater which contained 30 feet of $\frac{3}{4}$ inch copper pipe, double coiled, and entered the boiler at almost a boiling point. This boiler was said to be a fine steam generator, and, in case of repairs, could be easily got at by removing the bolts which connected the two flanges together. One other feature about this engine which differed from others, was its steam-supply-pipe which was made large and contained both the exhaust and the live steam, the latter passing down through a tube in the centre, while the exhaust steam passed up around the outside of the steam pipe which served to keep it hot, and finally passing out into the smoke stack.

This engine was built in a thorough and workmanlike manner, being finely finished and hung on platform springs. The weight, when loaded, was 6,000 lbs. It was in service in the Pittsburgh department for a number of years and was finally sold to Johnstown, Pa., where it did good service until the great flood which befell that city on May 31st, 1889, when it was swept away and entirely destroyed.

JOHN AGNEW — 1859.

John Agnew, the famous Hand Engine builder of Philadelphia, built three Steam Fire-Engines, the first of which was constructed for the "Northern Liberty" Engine Co. of that city, in 1859, and it was an exceedingly odd looking affair. The boiler was hori-

FAIRMOUNT ENGINE NO. 32.

Built by John Agnew.

zontal and of the "Demfield" patent, and was fitted with two smoke-stacks, one on either side. The pump, which was single, direct and double acting, with crosshead and connecting rod, lay horizontally upon the boiler, as did also the balance wheel. His other engines were similar in appearance to those built by Reanie & Neafie. The following are the dimensions of the engine built for the "Fairmount" Engine Co. of Philadelphia:

the pump, which was Parry's patent, was 4½ in. in diameter, steam cylinder 8½ in. in diameter, 15-in. stroke. The weight was 7,500 lbs. About the year 1867, Jacob L. Haupt succeeded Agnew, and built four or five steamers from designs of his own. These machines had two single acting pumps 4½ in. in diameter with 14-in. stroke, which were

PROTECTION ENGINE NO. 5, NEW BRUNSWICK, N. J.

Built by Jacob L. Haupt.

placed at the forward part of the boiler at the bottom; between which, and on line with them, was one steam cylinder measuring 9¾ in. in diameter. A link movement was used, and two large fly wheels, working close together, were attached to the main shaft. The frame was similar to that of the Harp tank, Amoskeag, only it was a double forging instead of a casting. A common tubular boiler was used. The weight of one of these engines was about 6,300 lbs.

ISAAC P. MORRIS & CO. — 1859.

The name of Isaac P. Morris as a Steam Fire-Engine builder is little known outside of Philadelphia, he having built but three engines. Possibly he may have made his fortune on these; but it is probable that he, like several other builders, knew when to

GOOD WILL ENGINE, PHILADELPHIA.
Built by I. P. Morris.

quit. The cut represents the "Good Will" engine, No. 20, of the Vol. Fire Dept. of Philadelphia, built in 1859, and for many years afterward used by Engine Co. No. 17 of the paid department. This engine was built from designs of Mr. Alexander McCausland of Philadelphia, and in appearance differed entirely from that of any other make. The boiler, which was tubular, stood very high, was vertically suspended from the frame about half way between the forward and rear wheels, the furnace door being on the right hand or working side of the engine. The steam cylinder, which was 10½ in. in diameter, with 15-in. stroke, was placed horizontally at the forward part of the engine, on top of which was the driver's seat. The pump, which measured 5½ by 15 in., was located at the rear of the boiler or pan end of the engine. The piston rod worked direct through a sleeve in the boiler to the steam cylinder. The balance wheel, which was worked by a crank motion, lay flat on top, between the boiler and steam cylinder. The weight was 9,550 lbs.

This machine was kept in constant use until 1888, when, after being capsized, it was condemned and broken up. The many years of duty which this engine performed in the heart of the city speaks well for an engine that was constructed at a period when they were known as novelties. The other two engines built by this firm were entirely different in design and resembled those built by Reanie and Neafie.

ETTENGER & EDMOND — 1859.

In the fall of 1859, Ettenger & Edmond, of Richmond, Va., built their first Steam Fire-Engine. These engines were built from designs of Mr. Alexander McCausland of Philadelphia. Their first machine was built for Messrs. Winans, Harrison & Winans of St. Petersburg, Russia, and was a credit to its builders.

BUILT BY ETTENGER & EDMOND.

The workmanship was first class as regards strength, beauty of finish and efficiency. The boiler was a vertical tubular, contracted at the waist, with an extensive heating surface, was rated as about 20 horse power and contained 163 $1\frac{1}{2}$ inch smoke tubes 3 feet 9 inches long. The entire machinery was secured to the frame in a horizontal position and embraced great simplicity and compactness. The steam cylinder was single and 9 inches in diameter, with the steam chest beneath. The valve was so arranged that in case any water worked over from the boiler, it would work its own way out without having to open the cylinder cocks. The valve was worked by an eccentric on the fly-wheel shaft in connection with a rock arm as on ordinary engines. The stroke was 15 inches. The pumps were of gun metal and set one above the other and were reciprocating in motion, the crosshead of the engine being made in such a way that the piston rod from the steam cylinder was fastened in the centre. The two pump pistons took hold, one above the other, below the steam piston, while the side or connecting rods took hold of the ends which projected over the sides of the frame and gave motion to the fly-wheel. One of the pumps — the lower one — was cast solid to the vacuum chamber; so that, no matter how much the engine was jolted over the streets, the vacuum chamber would always be tight. This arrangement of pump gave a chance for the suction valves to be placed between the pumps; so that the instant the engine changed its direction, the water was taken off the valves, leaving them free to act without any dead water on them. The valves were the ordinary click style and either one would fit in the place of the other. The pumps were each $3\frac{1}{4}$ inches in diameter, with same stroke as engine; each double acting. The body of the machine rested on six semi-elliptic springs and rode very easily. Its weight, all complete without wood and water, was 6,500 lbs. The rear wheels were 4 feet 9 inches high, front ones, 4 feet 6 inches, and it was easily drawn by two horses. The boiler was jacketed with Russia iron, with heavy brass bands. The fly-wheels were on either side of the air-chamber which was tall and handsomely shaped.

This engine was completed in 70 days. At a trial in Richmond, Va., this engine was drawn up to a fire plug on Main Street and the fire lighted. In ten minutes, an abundance of steam was made and the machinery put in motion. With a $1\frac{1}{8}$ inch nozzle, a stream was thrown high above the eagle on the American Hotel. A horizontal stream was then thrown down Main Street to a distance of 240 feet. It was then taken to the canal, and, while raising its own water, threw a $1\frac{1}{8}$ inch stream 240 feet, and a $1\frac{1}{2}$ inch stream 143 feet, and two $\frac{7}{8}$ inch streams 183 feet each.

This trial was made when everything was perfectly new and the boiler foaming from the grease or oil used in making it. At a subsequent trial at Philadelphia, it threw a $1\frac{1}{8}$ inch stream 263 feet.

This firm built only 5 fire engines, two of which went to St. Petersburg, Russia, and three were sold to the city of Richmond, Va., one of which was designed by H. P. Edmond and built vertical with 9 inch steam cylinder, 5 inch pump with 12-inch stroke. The boiler was similar to their others, only it contained 187 $1\frac{1}{2}$ inch tubes. This firm would probably have done a much more extensive business in fire-engine building, had it not been for the breaking out of the war at which time they had a large contract with the Russian government for engines to cost $3,500 each. This contract had to be stopped on account of the war. In 1877 they built their last steamer for Russia and then gave up that branch of their business.

J. B. JOHNSON — 1859.

J. B. Johnson, the steam fire-engine builder, was well known throughout New England. He at first commenced business at the shops of the Metropolitan Works, at South Boston, in 1859, but shortly afterward transferred his business to the works of McKay & Gallagher at East Boston, where his first engine, named "Antelope," was built. This

JOHNSON ENGINE CASCO NO. 5, PORTLAND, ME.
Built by J. B. Johnson.

machine, like all of his engines, with one exception, was horizontal, with one pump and one steam-cylinder, — the pump was $4\frac{1}{2}$ in. diameter, $9\frac{1}{2}$ in. stroke, the steam-cylinder $7\frac{1}{2}$ in. diameter, $9\frac{1}{2}$ in. stroke, — and weighed, when empty, 3,400 lbs., and when filled and ready to fire up, 3,900 lbs., which was considered in those days a very light engine.

This machine was tested at the City Hall, Boston, on Sept. 8, 1859. In four minutes from the time of applying the torch, the "Antelope" sounded a shrill whistle, and in two minutes after, with ten pounds of steam, water was passing through the leading hose. The stream gradually went up, and with fifteen pounds of steam reached the apex of the roof of the City Hall. With twenty pounds of steam, water reached to the height of the flag-staff; and with fifty-five pounds a good stream was sent several feet higher. At this

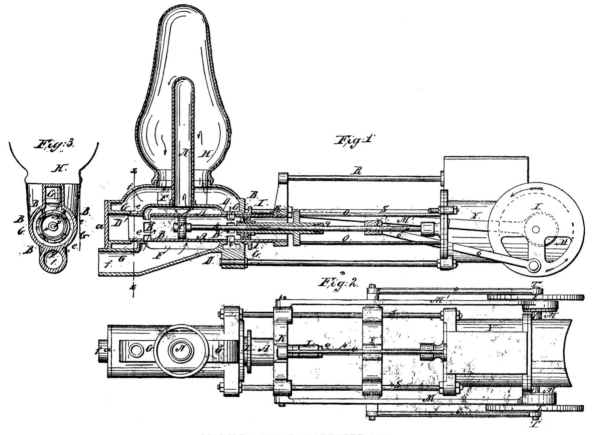

JOHNSON PUMP, PATENTED 1860.

point, through inattention, the fire became nearly extinct; but it was soon rekindled, and with a steam pressure of forty pounds, two $\frac{7}{8}$-in. streams were sent to the top of the staff. The trial closed by playing a $1\frac{1}{8}$-in. stream, with forty pounds of steam, which was handsomely thrown upon the flag-staff and over the roof of the Hancock House.

This engine was exhibited in several cities, and afterwards loaned on various occasions; but, I believe, was never sold.

Johnson's second engine was also built at the works of McKay & Gallagher, was sold to Salem, Mass., and was named for Chief-Engineer William Chase of that city. This was the last engine built by Johnson in Boston, as he removed his business, in the fall of '59, to the shops of the Portland Co.'s Works, at Portland, Me., where he settled down for business; and in the spring of 1860, the "Greyhound" was completed and tested at Charlestown Square, April 25. This engine weighed 4,025 lbs., and was rated as second class. It combined points of novelty and great efficiency with compactness and lightness. The steam power was derived from an upright tubular boiler, containing 214

JOHNSON'S LAST DESIGN.

sq. ft. of heating surface. From the boiler the engine and pump projected horizontally forward, being enclosed between two thin, wrought-iron frames, which served for guides for the crossheads. The double-acting pump, lying at the front of the engine, was $4\frac{1}{2}$ in. in diameter, was of composition, very handsomely finished, and of a very peculiar pattern, entirely different from any other. It was valveless, the pump-barrel being a working part of the pump, moving back and forth, opening and closing ports on about the same principle as a common steam-cylinder is operated. This pump-barrel was worked from the back part of the pump, having a crosshead attached, from which were two connecting-rods connected to the balance-wheels, which were on either side of the steam-cylinder, made of solid steel and worked by a double crank motion, which gave the pump-barrel a $3\frac{1}{4}$-in. slide; and on the reversing of the plunger stroke, which was 10 in., would close one set of ports and open the others. The pump was capable of making between 300 and 400 strokes per minute. The steam-cylinder was directly behind the pump, lying between and bolted to the frames before mentioned. Its diameter was 9 in., and stroke of piston 10 in. The front axle was connected with the engine by a transom bolt, fastened to one long semi-elliptic spring, one end of which was hung under the pump and the other end under the steam cylinder. From this axle the pole extended forward, and connected with this, was a self-acting brake arrangement, by which a very light pressure back upon the pole would set the brakes upon the wheels, and a pull forward would instantly loosen them again. She was also fitted with an iron tongue and a drag-rope to be drawn by hand. The hind-axle was bolted to two semi-elliptic springs, one on each side, these being fastened, one end to a hanger on the side of the boiler, the other end to a hanger on the pan behind the boiler. The forward wheels were 4 ft. 10 in., the rear ones 5 ft. 10 in. The pump was surmounted with a large air-chamber, with a silver-plated lantern at the top, and the finish of these, together with the brass and highly-polished iron work throughout, made a very beautiful engine. The suction-hose was attached to the front of the pump, and when not in use, was carried squirrel-tail fashion on brackets on the side.

In 1865, Mr. Johnson patented a new style engine, the balance-wheel lying flat and going round like a top. However, but one or two of these engines were built. Mr. Johnson gave up the business in 1869, having built about thirty machines. All, with the exception of one double vertical engine, were single and all of the horizontal style.

G. J. & J. L. CHAPMAN — 1860.

In looking over the various designs of different builds of Steam Fire-Engines, one cannot help noticing certain similarities of one make to another, going to show that, as a general rule, builders will copy from each other as far as it is policy for them to do so

HURRICANE NO. 13, PHILADELPHIA, PA.

Built by Chapman.

without boldly infringing on other patents. Such, however, cannot be said of G. J. & J. L. Chapman of Philadelphia, Pa., as their engines were built on an entirely new and novel plan; and, if they were not successful, they should at least have the credit of using their own ingenuity to the best of their ability.

This firm built only seven engines, the first two of which were constructed for the

" Fellowship " and " Assistance " Engine Companies of the Volunteer Fire Department of Philadelphia. The " Fellowship " was delivered and tested in December, 1860. At the trial she threw one stream, through a 1¼ inch nozzle, to the distance of 219 feet, and through two ⅞-inch nozzles water was forced to the distance of 195 feet. This engine was rated as third class, weighed 4,300 lbs. when loaded and cost $2,600.

As before stated, Chapman's engines were of a very peculiar design. The pumps were laid horizontally at the forward part of the machine and were two in number, both being single acting, varying from 4 to 4⅝ inches in diameter with from 12 to 16 inch stroke of piston. The steam cylinder, of which there was only one, was suspended from the frame near the boiler in a vertical position. The steam piston-rod worked vertically through the tophead of the cylinder, attached to which was a crosshead from which two connecting rods ran to the balance wheels on either side which worked the main crank shaft, to the cranks of which were attached two pump rods which worked horizontally and alternately. The boilers used were what is known as the " long tube boiler."

These engines were built in a very substantial and workmanlike manner and made a very pretty appearance. The first two machines were built different in their movement from the others, there being only one fly-wheel, while on the opposite side the connecting rod was attached to a small gear-wheel which in turn worked a larger one, to which was attached the crank shaft, the object being to have the pumps work slower than the steam piston. The stroke of pump was 16 inches while the steam stroke was only 10 inches. The piston rod, instead of passing through the steam cylinder, only connected with the piston, while below the cylinder were guides with sliding blocks.

CAMPBELL & WHITTIER — 1860.

The steam fire-engines built at the works of Campbell & Whittier at Roxbury, Mass., were constructed from plans designed by Mr. J. M. Stone of Manchester, N. H. These machines, however, did not become very popular and but three were made, two of which were sold to Roxbury, and were known, after annexation to Boston, as "Tremont Engine, No. 13," and "Dearborn Engine, No. 14." The other, I believe, went to Portsmouth, N. H. These engines were odd looking affairs. The boiler was located at the rear, was vertical, and of the tubular pattern. The steam cylinder and one double acting

TREMONT NO. 13. BUILT BY CAMPBELL & WHITTIER.

plunger pump were connected with the forward part of the boiler in a vertical position, the pump below the steam-cylinder and very close together, the piston-rod working directly through both, with a cross head on top, which was worked by a link motion. The air-chamber was of long, cylindrical shape, placed vertically and supported the pump and steam-cylinder on the opposite side from the boiler. The discharge gates were at the base of the air-chamber. The crank shaft was on top, receiving its support from two bearings, one on the boiler and the other on the top of the air-chamber. The balance-wheel was on the front end of the shaft and directly back of the driver's seat, which was on a crane-neck frame connected to the air-chamber. The pump was $5\frac{1}{2}$ inches in diameter with 12-inch stroke, inlets being on the side. The steam-cylinder was 9 inches in diameter, 12-inch stroke. They were hung on elliptical springs forward, and spiral springs behind. The weight of these engines was about 8,000 lbs.

(77)

WILLIAM JEFFERS — 1861.

William Jeffers, the famous engine builder, of Pawtucket, R. I., was born in the town of Milton, Mass., a short distance from Boston, in the year 1809. Mr. Jeffers was a man of large physical proportions, although considerably below the medium height. His hand engines, of which he built two styles, known as "side strokes" and "double deckers," had a national reputation, and the name "William Jeffers" was a familiar one

SINGLE PUMP JEFFERS ENGINE.

all over the country. In the year 1861, he turned his attention to the building of steamers and met with fair success. His double machines were made in one size only, while his single engines were built in two sizes. They were all of the vertical pattern and constructed in the most substantial manner. The steam cylinders received their support from the frame resting upon steel columns; this being an original idea, and afterwards patterned in a large degree by others. They were provided with patent cylindrical steam valves. Either crank or yoke motion was used, according to the fancy or desire of the purchasers. The boiler was steel, upright and tubular, of peculiar construction, with inverted smoke-box and furnace, with copper tubes. The inlets were on either side, but several were made, by order, to draft at the rear also.

The following are the dimensions of his double engine: steam-cylinders 9 in. in diameter, pumps $4\frac{3}{4}$ in. in diameter with $7\frac{1}{2}$-in. stroke of piston. The first size single engines had one steam-cylinder 9 in. in diameter and one pump $5\frac{1}{4}$ in. in diameter with $7\frac{1}{2}$-in. stroke, and weighed, when loaded and ready for service, about 8,000 lbs. Only

SINGLE ENGINE BUILT BY P. S. SKIDMORE.

one second-class machine was built, which had $3\frac{3}{4}$-in. pump, 7-in. steam-cylinder and $7\frac{1}{2}$-in. stroke.

Mr. Jeffers continued the business of building steam fire-engines until 1874, at which time he had constructed 63 machines, when the hard times compelled him to make an assignment. In December, 1875, he sold out his business to P. S. Skidmore of Bridgeport, Conn., and met his obligations in an honorable manner.

Wm. Jeffers died at his residence in Pawtucket, R. I., of apoplexy, in 1879, in the 70th year of his age. Mr. Skidmore continued the building of the Jeffers engines at Bridgeport, but did not meet with much success. He constructed only eight machines, when, in 1878, fire destroyed most of the patterns, and the business was discontinued.

CLAPP & JONES — 1862.

Clapp & Jones of Hudson, N. Y., can well be rated as one of the few firms which were successful builders of Steam Fire-Engines. They commenced building in 1862, and, up to the present time, have turned out over 600 machines, which, in most cases, have given good satisfaction.

Their first engines were built straight frame, horizontal, and both single and double pumps. They were classed in five sizes; the fifth, or smallest size, weighing but 3,200 lbs. These engines were designed by Mr. M. R. Clapp, and every engine was constructed under his direct supervision. These machines were what, in common phrase, is called "Piston engines." The machinery was arranged so that the connections between the steam and water cylinders, were direct through piston-rods, and not through shafts and gear as in some engines, nor through cranks and connecting rods as in others. The boilers were vertical, with both water and fire tubes. The fire tubes extended from the crown-sheet of the fire-box up through the top of the shell. The water-tubes were pendent from the crown-sheet and in rows. The two outside rows extended nearly to the bottom of the fire-box; and the others, about half the length, were in the centre. These tubes were so constructed as to give a circulation to the water by placing inside a triangular partition. The connections of the steam-pipes to the engine were made so that they were not exposed to the cold air. The pumps were so arranged that by taking off the heads (which could be done in ten minutes) the valves were taken out at the same time. The suction-hose always remained connected with the pump, thereby making one less connection in getting to work. All the smaller sizes were usually made to be run by hand and the larger ones fitted with pole for horses and seat for driver; but they were all so made that they could very easily be changed for horses or to be run by hand. Brakes were attached to all. Those on the hand machine were operated from the fuel pan; on the horse machines, from the driver's foot-board. They were hung on elliptical springs forward and rubber behind. A fifth-class engine of this style had $4\frac{5}{8}$ inch pump, with 7-inch stroke; steam-cylinder $7\frac{1}{2}$ inches in diameter, 7-inch stroke.

Some years ago, this firm, to keep pace with the times and satisfy everybody, changed their style and commenced building them upright and crane-neck. Of these, they finished six sizes, the largest of which is rated as extra. No. 1 weighed 8,500 lbs., steam cylinders 9 inches by 8-inch stroke; pump cylinders $5\frac{1}{2}$ inches and 8-inch stroke; with a water capacity of 1,000 gallons per minute. The first, second and third are double pump, fourth and fifth single. The boiler on these engines is quite different from their old style and is called a "Sectional Coil Tube" boiler, having, in place of the drop tubes,

MODERN DOUBLE CLAPP & JONES ENGINE.

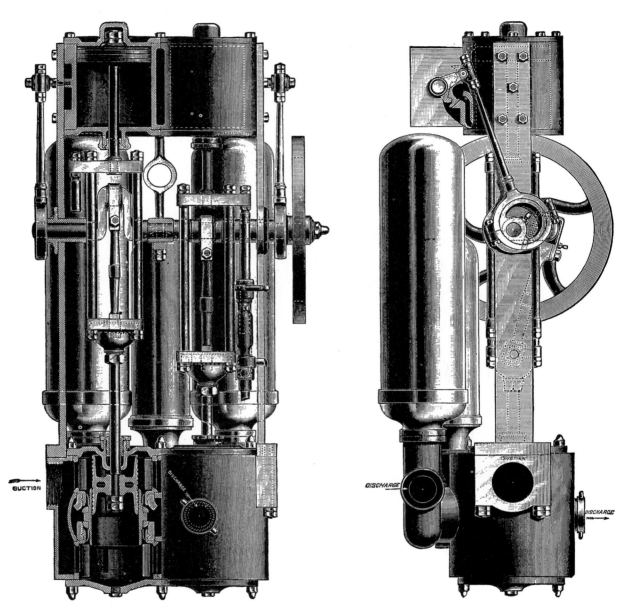

SECTION OF CLAPP & JONES DOUBLE VERTICAL ENGINE.

a series of coil tubes made of copper. They are in the form of a spiral coil, allowing for expansion from heat and contraction from cold. The spiral bend is enough to leave room for five others of the same size between; so that there are six of these coils in each circular row. The number of rows is determined by the size of the boiler and the amount of steam required. Each coil is connected with the lower tube-sheet by screw-joints all right hand, an angle-elbow being used to get the short bend at the end. The

CLAPP & JONES VILLAGE ENGINE.

tube then makes about one turn around the fire-box and is joined to the side-sheet with a similar union to that used at the upper end.

The latest addition to this boiler is a Fire Deflector, as there was a space of considerable diameter in the centre of the fire-box, and the tendency of this space, if left unoccupied, acted as a flue, causing an excessive amount of heat to pass up through the central fire-tubes, resulting in their undue expansion as compared with the other tubes, and loosening the joints of the latter in the top-head.

To overcome this difficulty, as well as to effect a more uniform passage of heat through the fire-tubes, and at the same time provide additional water circulation passages and heating surface in the hottest part of the fire-box, they placed what is called a "Water Circulating Fire Deflector," which occupies the space in the centre of the fire-box within the coil-tubes, and consists of a number of sections which are connected in series vertically, so as to reach from the crown-sheet, into which the deflector is screwed, to the bottom of the spiral coils, where connection is made with the water-leg of the boiler.

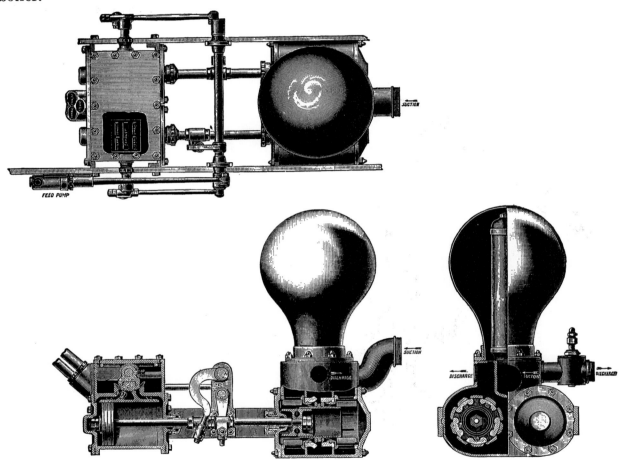

SECTIONS OF CLAPP & JONES VILLAGE ENGINE.

The pump is of novel construction and made entirely of composition (copper and tin) having high tensile strength. It is so constructed as to require no leather or other forms of packing to make friction for the plunger. The pump-heads are simply cages, fitted with inlet and outlet valves of simple form of construction, doing away with the necessity of spiral springs to bring the valves back to their places, their own elasticity being sufficient to quickly and firmly seat them. The machinery is so arranged that the connections between the steam and water-cylinders are direct through piston-rods which are moved by a crank motion and connecting rod.

SECTION OF CLAPP & JONES PUMP.

SECTION OF CLAPP & JONES PUMP.

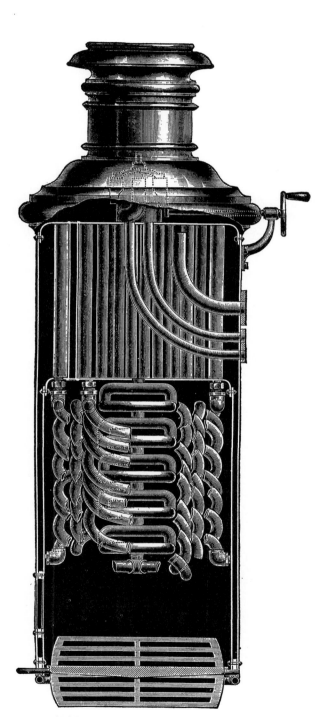

MODERN CLAPP & JONES BOILER.

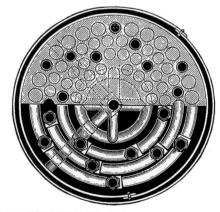

BOTTOM SECTION OF CLAPP & JONES BOILER.

FIRE DEFLECTOR.

A short time ago this company consolidated with the following Steam Fire-Engine builders: Silsby of Seneca Falls, N. Y., Button of Waterford, N. Y., and Ahrens of Cincinnati, Ohio, which combination is now known as the " American Fire Engine Company."

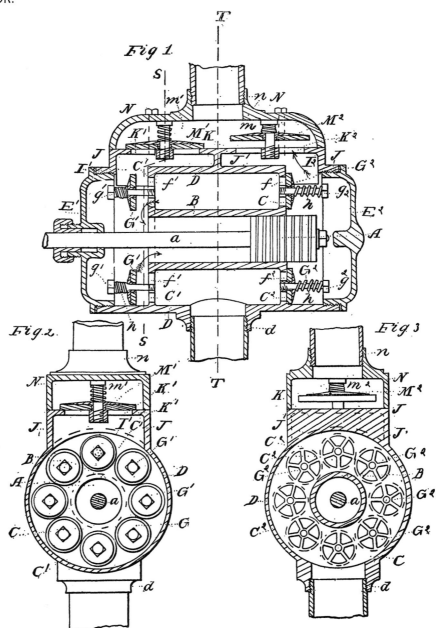

HORIZONTAL PUMP, PATENTED BY M. R. CLAPP, 1865.

L. BUTTON — 1862.

Foremost among the pioneers in the manufacture of Fire-Engines, stands Mr. L. Button, for whom was named the famous Button Fire-Engine Works at Waterford, Saratoga Co., New York.

This concern is one of the oldest and most extensive fire apparatus builders on this continent. They not alone occupy this unchallenged prominence among the engine

WARREN NO. 12, BOSTON, MASS.
Built by Button & Blake.

manufacturers of North America, but their position as representative inventors and producers, is established over the entire globe. It is, indeed, a great honor, but the laurels fall gracefully, and there are none who should be envious enough to say they have been misplaced.

L. Button first commenced building hand-engines in 1834; and they were received with great enthusiasm by firemen everywhere. Improvements were rapidly made on these machines, and, notwithstanding the introduction of steam-engines into many departments, they were used in preference. The reputation enjoyed by the Button Co. for the records made by the apparatus of their make, is one of which they may well feel proud; and it is not without some justice that they claim the championship for the

(87)

best hand fire-engine made.   This they base upon the fact that during the last twenty-five years, these engines have taken more than two-thirds of all the prizes at musters and challenge tests.

When, some thirty years ago, steam engines became a necessity in large cities, Messrs. Button & Blake turned their attention to this phase of the business, and in 1862

MODEL OF L. BUTTON & SON.

their first steam fire-engine was completed.   It was quite a curiosity at that time, and people went miles to see it.   Prominent fire chiefs from all over the United States visited the works at Waterford, and commended the apparatus.   This machine was finally sold to the city of Battle Creek, Michigan, and, for many years, fought the fiery element.

The first engines were straight frame, with single $6\frac{3}{8}$-in. pump and $11\frac{1}{4}$-in. steam-cylinder, which lay horizontally on the frame and very close together.   The piston-rod was in one piece, and worked direct through steam-cylinder with a 9-in. stroke.   The pump was directly over the forward axle, and surmounted with a large double air-chamber.   The suction-hose was connected with the pump and carried squirrel-tail fashion.   The boilers were large and of the waist pattern.   These engines were hung on elliptical springs and weighed about 7,500 lbs.   Mr. Button, like all progressive men, from time to time made vast improvements, both in style and construction of his engines; and those of to-day do not resemble in the least his machines of 1863.   These engines are built at present in six sizes.   The first class or largest size will weigh 7,000 lbs., exclusive of water and fuel; second class, 6,000; third class, 5,000; fourth class, 4,000; fifth class, 3,000; sixth class, 2,500.

These engines are all of the crane-neck pattern. The three smaller sizes differ in construction from the three larger ones, as the pumps and working parts are over the forward axle, while in the larger sizes they are placed below the frame and close up to the boiler, which is upright and of the tubular pattern, with submerged combustion

MODERN DOUBLE BUTTON ENGINE.

chamber. The flues are of copper, and the steam-chamber and smoke-flue are so arranged as to obviate all difficulty arising from the unequal expansion of iron and copper when heated, as these boilers are made in two parts and are connected together with water-tubes, which keep the bottom of the top section or combustion chamber covered with water at all times. These boilers can be taken apart and put together without removing rivets or breaking packed joints. The flue-sheets are so formed and arranged that all scale deposits or mud sediment, which are always to be found in boilers, are driven by the heat into the leg of the boiler, where they can be removed through the cleaning holes.

The flues are securely held at both ends in heavy head-sheets and they are protected from injury by the inside shell of the boiler and are always covered with water. The pumps are cast in a single piece, without packed partitions, and are made of the best bronze metal, the water nowhere coming in contact with iron. The water-ways are direct and large. The valves are on bronze seats, easily separated from the pump-casting, and are readily accessible for inspection or repairs. They are of rubber, with bronze bushings, and are of the size and proportion best adapted for the purpose. The double pumps on these machines are made by casting two pumps in one piece side by side, having no packed partitions, and are fitted in exactly parallel lines to two steam-cylinders with adjacent heads in one piece so they cannot be out of line. This renders the parts of the engine practically a unit and free from the chance of becoming disabled by accident to running-gear, expansion from heat or strain from pressure. The steam-chest and ports are under the cylinders, so as to completely drain them of condensed water, and each steam-valve is moved by the opposite piston by means of a direct lever, without the intervention of balance-wheels, crankshaft, link-blocks, connecting-rods, eccentrics, gearing or any revolving parts. All the movable parts of the engine are reciprocating. In short, they have no machinery but the straight piston and valve-rods, except in their smaller size of engine, where balance-wheels and connecting-rods are used. The pumps are all double-acting, and take their water from the side. The pumps of a first-class engine measure 7 inches in diameter, $4\frac{1}{2}$ inch stroke. All the engines built by this firm were horizontal with but one exception. It was a beautiful, double, vertical machine and is now owned by the American Fire Engine Company and used as a relief engine. It was first exhibited at the New York State Fireman's Convention at Troy in 1887. Up to the present time, there have been over one hundred engines built by this firm. For some

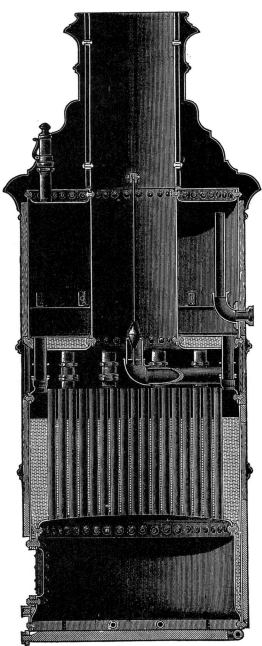

MODERN BUTTON BOILER.

years, Mr. Holroyd & Co. have had charge, but a short time ago this company consolidated with the following steam fire-engine builders: Silsby of Seneca Falls, N. Y., Ahrens of Cincinnati, Ohio, Clapp & Jones of Hudson, N. Y., and are now known as the "American Fire Engine Company."

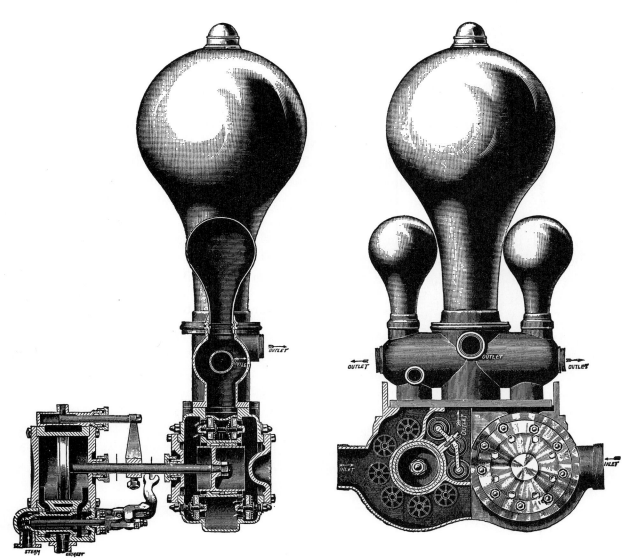

SECTION OF BUTTON ENGINE.

JOHN A. IVES & BROTHER — 1864.

The engines built by John A. Ives & Bro. and Ives & Son of Baltimore, Md., had the reputation of being very durable and efficient. The Baltimore Fire Department at one time had several of these engines in the service which gave entire satisfaction. These machines were built in several sizes and were constructed double vertical with crane-neck and single horizontal straight frame. The following are the dimensions of one of their second-class single pump horizontal engines. Height from floor to top of smoke-stack 8 feet 4 inches. Length over all, including tongue, 21 feet. Diameter of boiler 32 inches. Diameter of steam-cylinder 9 inches. Diameter of pump 5 inches. Length of stroke 12 inches, direct acting, with crosshead, connecting rod and balance wheel movement. Weight, without water and fuel, 6,500 lbs.

The frames of these horizontal engines were made of boiler iron and cylindrical in form, one end of which was flanged and bolted to the boiler in such a manner that it could easily be removed in case of necessity. This frame or cylinder also served as a feed-water tank. The pump and steam-cylinder were placed horizontally upon the tank, the base of the cylinders being so formed as to saddle the tank to which they were firmly bolted. The pump, being at the forward end, was made of gun metal and was double acting, having eight brass suction-valves, four on each side, and four discharge valves, opening into the air vessels, to which a double discharge valve, having one opening on the inside and two on the outside, was attached for the purpose of using two lines of hose. Each of these discharge gates was furnished with a stop valve, which was opened and closed by a lever, and as the pump valves covered very large and direct openings, the engines could be run at a very high speed, without any jar and without the pumps running away from the water. The valves were also so conveniently arranged as to be capable of being cleaned, renewed or repaired with little trouble. The suction hose was connected at all times at the forward end of the tank, and when not in use, was carried squirrel-tail fashion. The boilers were upright and tubular, with conical smoke-box, submerged combustion chamber and contracted waist. The feed-water was heated before entering the boiler, by being passed through a copper coil inside of the smoke-stack. A dump grate was also used, which admitted of the fire being drawn at short notice if required. These boilers, in like manner as the steam cylinder, were jacketed and banded with German silver or brass which gave them a very neat and ornamental appearance.

This firm discontinued the building of Steam Fire-Engines in 1884.

BUILT BY IVES & SON.

R. J. GOULD — 1865.

Mr. R. J. Gould of Newark, N. J., was a noted Steam Fire-Engine builder of that state. He commenced the building of steamers in 1865. His machines were built in five sizes, the first and second being double, and the third, fourth and fifth single. The first class weighed 6,500 lbs., second class 5,400 lbs., pumps 4½ inches in diameter, steam-cylinder 7 inches diameter, 8-inch stroke, third class 4,200 lbs., fourth class 3,800 lbs. and fifth class 3,000 lbs. All were link-motion and crane-neck, unless otherwise ordered. The boiler was what is known as a vertical tubular with submerged smoke-flues. The fire-box was made tapering, giving an increased area of grate, the water-leg being larger at the top than at the bottom, which the inventor claimed gave a better cir-culation than if made straight. The smoke-box was conical in form and made of one sheet. The quickest steaming made by one of these boilers is claimed by the Eagle Steam Fire Engine, No. 7, of New Orleans, La., which raised steam from cold water and turned over in 2 minutes 20 seconds and forced water through 100 feet of hose in 2 minutes 50 seconds. The feed-water was heated by passing through the fire-box. The steam-cylinder and pumps, which were double-acting, were attached to the frame of their vertical engines by forged studs or columns which were firmly fastened to the frame. The cylinders were braced to the boiler and frame and both set as near the boiler as was consistent. The piston-rods were connected together with a yoke for link-blocks in the usual manner. The steam-cylinders of the double engines were in one casting, with the steam-chest opening in the front. In the single cylinders, the steam-chest was on the side; so, in either case, it was easy to get at the valves when necessary; which, however, was seldom needed as the valves could never get out of position, the eccentrics being forged solid with the crank-shaft. The pumps were made of composi-tion and contained side-valves which were easily reached by taking off the bottom head of the pump and dropping down the valve-plate and cylinder. Water could be taken in at either side of the engine and the suction-hose kept attached, ready for use at all times if desired. These engines were mounted on wooden wheels and set on the well-known "Hibbard" spiral springs, and were models of beauty when the price was paid for extra finish.

The best play made by one of these machines through a single line of 100 feet of hose was 354 feet 4 inches.

The following is from the Newark *Daily Advertiser* of Aug. 24, 1874: "A new Steam Fire-Engine built by R. J. Gould of this city for the Fame Hose Company No. 1 of Wilmington, Del., was tried on Saturday from the river, foot of Jackson Street, in presence of a committee of the company and a number of our own firemen and others interested in such matters. The committee of the Fame Hose Company have given the following certificate:—

" This is to certify that the first-class engine, built by R. J. Gould of Newark, N. J., for the Fame Hose Company of Wilmington, Del., was tested this day on Passaic River with the following results: first throw 1½ inch nozzle 328 feet 6 inches; second throw

MECHANIC ENGINE NO. 7, MOBILE, ALABAMA.

2 inch nozzle 209 feet; third throw 2¼ inch nozzle 205 feet; fourth throw 2 streams 1¼ inch nozzles 262 feet; fifth throw one 1½ inch nozzle 354 feet 4 inches. Time of steaming, 5 lbs. in 4½ minutes; 10 lbs. in 4¾ minutes; 15 lbs. in 5 minutes. Time of running 2½ hours.

WILLIAM H. QUINN,
JOHN L. RILEY,
MARTIN ELLIOT,
THOMAS BLANKEN,
JOHN STRATNER,

Committee of Fame Hose Company."

Mr. John N. Dennisson, the noted hand-engine builder, commonly called " Pop " by his acquaintances, was, for a number of years, connected with this establishment, and was, in fact, the inventor of these engines, which were built from his patents; the crane-neck style of frame being one of his ideas. Mr. Dennisson was in business for some time in building engines in Newark, N. J., and in Reading, Penn., and guaranteed his machines against any other make of the same weight in the country. He built in five sizes and they were constructed single and double, horizontal and vertical; the heaviest weighing

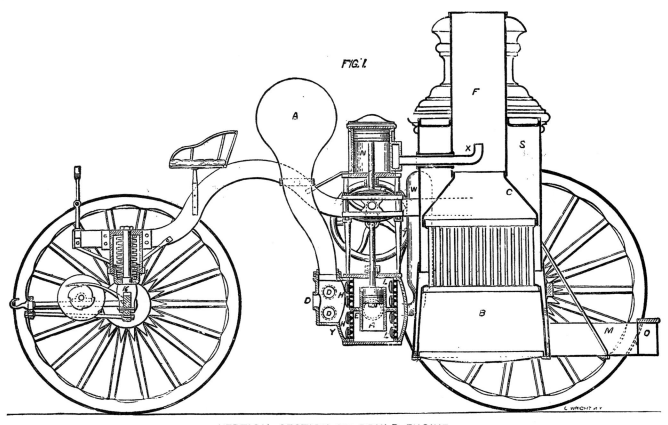

VERTICAL SECTION OF GOULD ENGINE.

6,800 lbs., and the lightest only 2,500 lbs. In the spring of 1878, he tested a third class single engine weighing only 3,932 lbs. at Trenton, N. J., with the following results, which speak well for his small machines:—

First throw 287 feet using $1\frac{1}{8}$ inch nozzle; second throw 260 feet using $1\frac{1}{4}$ inch nozzle. The third test was two lines with $1\frac{1}{16}$ inch and $\frac{3}{4}$ inch nozzles, when water was thrown to the distance of 236 feet.

Mr. Dennisson died in 1887, at which time he was blind and helpless. The Gould Company sold out their business in 1875 to Mr. B. S. Nichols & Co. of Burlington, Vt., with the entire rights, including patents, tools, etc., who continued to build the same.

One of the handsomest and best engines turned out by Mr. Nichols was built for the "Mechanic's Fire Engine Company No. 7" of Mobile, Ala. The following is from a Mobile paper of May, 1877 : —

NO. SEVEN'S NEW ENGINE.

Among the attractions of the fair for the last two days, one of the greatest was the new steamer for Mechanic's Fire Company No. 7. It is a third class Gould and the first one of the kind and style ever built. Light, it weighs 5,050 lbs. ready for service, with

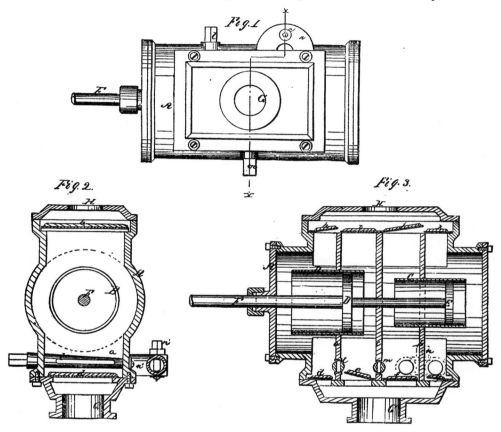

HORIZONTAL PUMP PATENTED BY J. N. DENNISSON, 1866.

two cocks of water about 5,400 lbs. It is a model in its finish and appointments and is the handsomest piece of workmanship of its kind in this country. The axle, crane-necks and all of the iron work are nickel-plated. The boiler is covered with German silver. The pumps, fly-wheels and other parts are of polished brass. It has patent side-lights, a chime of three whistles and a gong which is struck by a stop pushed by the driver's foot. It has two nickel plated steam gauges and a water gauge, as well as a heavily plated locomotive clock. It has double cylinders and pumps. Enough of the natural color of the engine is left to make a rich contrast with the nickel-plated portions. The coal-pan is made of brass, nickel-plated and ornamented with a rich moulding which forms a panel on both sides and in front. Within the latter is the name "Mechanic's 7," in raised letters; and upon the upper edge is an ornamental railing. Another beautiful feature is the signal-lantern, which surmounts the air-chamber. This is of shield shape. Upon one glass is the motto of No. 7 — "Independence, Usefulness our Aim," with a mechanic's strong right arm in the centre. Two of the other glasses are green, bearing the name and number of the steamer, "Mechanic's No. 7." The other glass is wine-color and has Erin's harp surmounted with shamrock leaves. The whole lantern is heavily silver-plated and handsomely ornamented with gold trimmings. On the top of each corner is an eagle and immediately under each at the bottom is a lion's head. A beautifully proportioned figure of a fireman surmounts the whole. The steamer was built by Messrs. B. S. Nichols & Co., of Burlington, Vt., and was sold through their agent, Capt. Ed. Flood of New Orleans and is the third he has ordered and sold within the past few months. There are six of these steamers in use in New Orleans and suburbs, and, as fast as they are known, they take the lead in all cities. The manufacturers have been running full shops all the

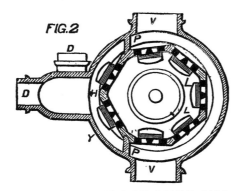

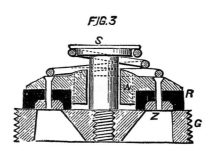

HORIZONTAL SECTION OF GOULD PUMP.   GOULD PUMP VALVE.

past winter to supply orders, one of which was recently sent to Europe. We think the engine does great credit to the building committee and we shall expect to hear her musical chime at every fire and hear a good report of her work. The Building Committee are James Flanagan, Chairman, S. A. Leonard, Joseph Cahill, C. Skelly and Thomas Jones. In this connection, we may say that this is the third time that Mr. Flanagan has been chairman of a like committee for a like purpose. The price paid for this beautiful steamer was $4,600. It was awarded a diploma and a silver medal at the fair. The official test by the Building Committee took place yesterday at the foot of St. Louis Street. The judges were Wm. S. Foster, Wm. Keyland, J. R. Williams, H. G. Kearns, and T. M. English. From the time the fire was lit until the whistle blew was 3 minutes 25 seconds. There were ten pounds steam pressure in 4 minutes, twenty in 6 minutes, thirty in 6 minutes 30 seconds, forty in 7 minutes, fifty in 7 minutes 30 seconds, sixty in 8 minutes 12½ seconds, seventy in 8 minutes 30 seconds, and eighty in 8 minutes 55 seconds. The time passing water through 100 feet of hose from nozzle, 5 minutes 57½ seconds, 50 feet, 6 minutes 57 seconds, 100 feet, 7 minutes 15 seconds. The distance thrown through 100 feet of hose with 1⅛ inch nozzle was 263 feet 5 inches, through 1¼ inch nozzle, 266 feet 5 inches, through 1³⁄₁₆ inch nozzle, 282 feet 11 inches and through 1½ inch nozzle, 184 feet 1 inch. The distance that two streams were thrown simultaneously through 100 feet of hose with 1 inch nozzle was 223 feet 6 inches. The next test was throwing one stream with 1 inch nozzle through 500 feet of hose. The stream reached 180 feet when the hose burst. The tests were satisfactory to the committee and to all of No. 7's men who were there, also to those of the large crowd present who were familiar with steam-engines. The throw was the best ever made in the United States by any third-class engine. The wind affected the throw, especially the cross winds, making a difference of at least ten feet.

Mr. Nichols gave up the building of steam fire-engines in 1879.

NORTHERN LIBERTY NO. 7, NEWARK, N. J.
Built by John N. Dennisson.

HUNNEMAN & CO. — 1866.

Joseph H. and John C. Hunneman, the veteran hand fire-engine builders of Boston, are known, by reputation, the world over. The firm of Hunneman & Co. was established by William Cooper Hunneman in the year 1792, and he conducted the business until his death. Then his sons, William and Samuel, took charge and carried on a large business for many years. Both died some time ago, and John C. (son of Samuel) and Joseph H. Hunneman succeeded them.

Their first steam fire-engine was built in the year 1866. The foreman of the shop was Mr. E. B. Jucket, a fine mechanic and very ingenious man. This engine was sold to the (at that time) town of Somerville, Mass., in 1866, for the sum of $4,500. The original cost to build was $7,000. This machine proved to be one of the best that they ever built, and was considered in her day to be as handsome an engine as there was in the state.

The boiler was of the vertical, tubular pattern, submerged flues, and contained 246 iron smoke tubes, $1\frac{1}{4}$ inches in diameter and 18 inches in length, which were screwed in the top sheet and expanded in the bottom head. The boiler was encased in an elegant brass jacket of a fluted design. The pumps and steam cylinders were double and of the plunger type, link motion, and placed vertical about 1 foot from the boiler, receiving their support wholly from the frame of the engine. The crank shaft was in two parts, with a balance wheel on both, which came face to face on the inside and were bolted together. The idea of this was, in case one side of the machine should become disabled, by removing the bolt, the side not injured could be worked singly, as there was an independent throttle for that purpose. The steam cylinders measured $6\frac{1}{2}$ inches in diameter with 8 inch stroke — pumps 4 inches in diameter with the same stroke as steam cylinder. The pumps were made of brass and were designed by Mr. Jucket. They were so arranged, that, by simply unscrewing the bottom heads, the valve beds and cylinders could be removed in a minute's time. The valves were at the top and bottom. This was the only pump of this design that was ever placed on their engines, owing to an alleged infringement on the Amoskeag pump. All of his other pumps had side valves. The frame of the engine was straight and very finely polished. The same can be said of the springs ; in fact, every part of the iron work was finished up and shone like a mirror. The inlet was at the rear of the machine, from which was attached the suction hose in squirrel-tail fashion. The outlets were two in number, and protruded through the feed-water tank at the forward part of the engine. This tank was square in shape, handsomely painted and bound in brass. The wheels were very high, the front ones measuring 5 feet 2 inches, and the rear ones 5 feet 5 inches in diameter. The air chamber was copper and of balloon shape, surmounted with a signal light. The total weight was 6,666 lbs., and could be drawn by two horses with ease. This engine was delivered May 26, 1866, and tested in Union Square, Somerville, with good results. On the 15th of June following, she was again tested at the United States Navy Yard, Charlestown, Mass., competing against a Jeffers and an Amoskeag engine, defeating both. The best play this machine ever made was through a single line of hose, playing a horizontal stream

SOMERVILLE NO. I, SOMERVILLE, MASS.
Hunneman's First Steamer.

262 feet. This engine is still in existence at St. Charles, Ill., where it was taken by Mr. H. M. Young, who bought it from a junk dealer, and who tried to induce the town to purchase it as they had no fire protection, but to no avail. Shortly after, in the year 1895, a large fire broke out which threatened the destruction of the whole town, whereupon Mr. Young ordered out the old war horse and put her to work, and in a very short time, two powerful streams were knocking the fire right and left as in days of yore, when suddenly one of the cylinder heads was blown off. This accident would wholly

disable almost any other make of engine, but after almost 30 years of duty, her peculiar construction came in play. Quickly her balance wheels were disconnected, and with only one pump and steam cylinder, it is said that she saved the town after over $70,000 worth of property had been destroyed. This is one of a few cases where an engine had been consigned to the junk heap and afterwards proved to be worth her weight in gold.

Hunneman built several engines later. They were all vertical and built single and double, crane neck and straight frame. Several of them were used in the Boston Fire Department. The firm suspended business in 1883. Mr. A. S. Jackson has since occupied their old office on Union St., Boston, and deals in Fire Department Supplies. On the morning of December 14th, 1887, Mr. Joseph H. Hunneman was found dead in his bed — death probably caused from heart disease. John C. Hunneman is still alive, and in the " Hub."

COLE BROTHERS — 1867.

The celebrated firm of Cole Brothers, of Pawtucket, R. I., did quite an extensive business in the manufacture of steam fire-engines between the years 1867 and 1880.

Their engines were all of the vertical plunger pattern, and were made both single and double, of which there were three classes, and were constructed to be drawn by horse or hand. Cole Brothers' claim for a vertical engine over a horizontal one, was, that

COLE BROTHERS DOUBLE ENGINE.

the wear is equal on all sides of the cylinders. They also claimed a great improvement in case the engine should have to go to draft, which consisted of a siphon running from the pump inlet up to the forward part of the engine to which the suction hose was connected. The water would always remain in this pipe, unless pumped out, which made it a self-charger.

The piston-rods were made of one continuous piece of steel instead of being in two

(103)

parts, and would not stick on the centres or cramp the sliding-box, which causes extra friction. The boiler was of an improved tubular style, which consisted of a double cone in the top, through which all the feed-water was pumped, so that it passed into the boiler hot. By this arrangement, not only was strength added to the top of the boiler, but a great saving of fuel was effected.

The wheels were made of wood, or iron, as desired. The pumps were of a very peculiar pattern and had all of the valves on the bottom plate and could be examined by simply unscrewing a cap. The steam and water cylinders on their double engines were placed in line, one before the other, instead of transversely as in other engines, which enabled the engineer to have perfect control over all the working parts of the machine without changing his position. They could be very easily disconnected and run singly. Both cylinders were placed in the centre of the bed, suspended in place by iron columns. The frame was straight, but made narrower than that of other engines, so that the machine could be turned around in as small a space as possible.

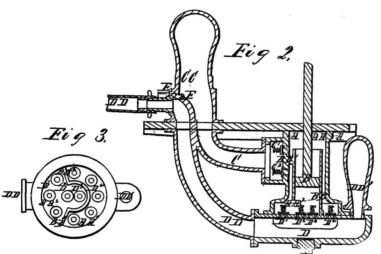

COLE BROTHERS PUMP.

The 1st class engine weighed about 6,500 lbs.; 2d class, 5,500 lbs.; 3d class, 4,500 lbs.; and they cost from $4,000 to $5,000. The first steamer was built by this firm in 1867, and was partially designed by George A. Saunders and George Baker, two former employees of William Jeffers, the engine builder.

This machine was sold to the city of Utica, N. Y., where it was used for many years. One of their best single engines was the "Rough and Ready," No. 2, built for Pawtucket, R. I., and was known as a third class, or the smallest built by this firm. It weighed 4,600 lbs., had a boiler $31\frac{1}{2}$ inches in diameter, with 252 one and a quarter inch tubes, 16 inches long. The steam cylinder was $9\frac{1}{2}$ inch diameter, and 8 inch stroke. It had one brass double-acting plunger pump, $5\frac{1}{2}$ inch diameter, stroke same as steam-cylinder. It raised 20 lbs. of steam in 3 minutes, 10 seconds, from the time of lighting fire. It is known to have thrown a horizontal stream 264 feet through a $1\frac{1}{8}$ inch nozzle. This machine cost $5,000, and was very beautifully finished.

The double engines manufactured by this firm had steam-cylinders $7\frac{1}{2}$ inches in diameter and 8 inch stroke, pumps $4\frac{3}{8}$ inches in diameter and 8 inch stroke. Cole Brothers constructed about 60 steam fire-engines. Of late years they have not built many, most of their work in that line being on repairing old engines and replacing boilers.

AHRENS — 1868.

The Ahrens Manufacturing Company, of Cincinnati, Ohio, is the largest firm engaged in the manufacture of Steam Fire-Engines in the West, and their machines are spoken of very highly by those using them. Over 700 of them have been sold. These works were originally owned by Latta, the famous inventor and builder of Steam Fire-Engines, who sold out the business in 1863 to Lane & Bodley. They built 7 or 8 machines from Latta's patterns, and gave up the business in 1868 to the Ahrens Manu-

SINGLE PUMP AHRENS.

facturing Company, who immediately made vast improvements over the old styles, finding for them a ready market.

These engines are all built vertical, with single and double pumps. The special feature of their machines is their boiler, which differs entirely from that of any other, as it has no smoke tubes and is known as a coil boiler, the boiler itself being only a shell, inside of which is placed a coil of pipes which run horizontally back and forth in the inside, and connected at the top and bottom of the shell, the fire passing around the outside of the tubes containing the water, and it is claimed that steam can be made from

MODERN DOUBLE AHRENS ENGINE.

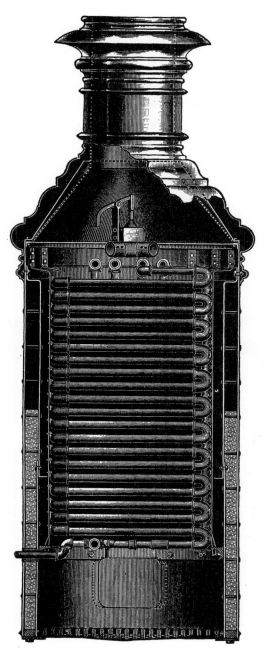

MODERN AHRENS BOILER.

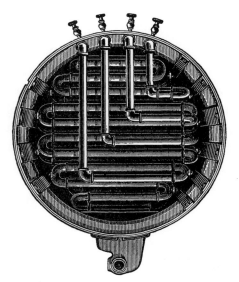

TOP VIEW OF AHRENS BOILER.

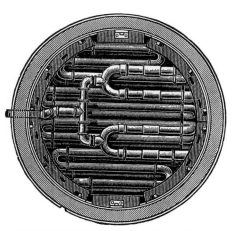

BOTTOM VIEW OF AHRENS BOILER.

cold water and a stream thrown inside of four minutes from time of lighting fire. In this boiler, the water is drawn from the shell by a circulating pump and forced into the coils at the bottom, passing through the hot coils and returning to the boiler at the top. Should repairs be needed, by simply breaking joints at top and bottom and removing a few side bolts, this coil can be easily removed. The steam cylinders and pumps of these machines are not attached to the boiler, but are separated therefrom sufficiently to allow every opportunity to get at each and every part. The steam-cylinders are of the ordinary slide-valve type. These engines are built on the " Scotch-yoke " style of movement. The yokes are forged from the solid, and the faces of the same are lined with oil tempered steel plates ; said plates are easily removed and replaced should it become necessary. All connections, both steam and water, are made outside of the boiler. The

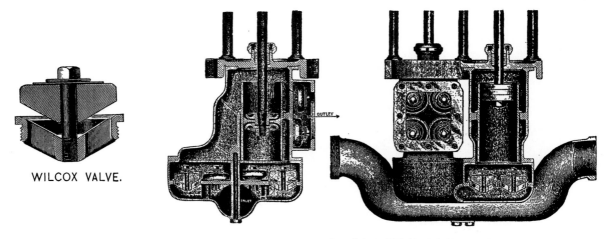

WILCOX VALVE.

SECTION OF AHRENS PUMP.

pumps are double acting and very simple, having four drafting valves on the bottom, and four forcing valves on the side. Gun-metal is used in all parts coming in contact with water. These engines are made in eight sizes. The largest six are made with double pumps and cylinders, "crane-neck" style, hung on equalizing platform springs forward, and half elliptical springs in the rear. The two smaller sizes are built with straight frames, and have single cylinder and pump, with half elliptic springs front and rear.

A first-class machine, special size, weighs 8,700 lbs.; steam cylinders, $8\frac{3}{4}$ inch diameter, 8 inch stroke, pumps, $5\frac{1}{2}$ inch diameter, 8 inch stroke. The eighth, or smallest size, weighs 3,200 lbs.; steam cylinder, $6\frac{1}{2}$ inch diameter, 7 inch stroke, pump, 4 inch diameter, 7 inch stroke. In 1891, this firm became consolidated with the following steam fire-engine builders : Silsby, of Seneca Falls, N. Y.; Button, of Waterford, N. Y.; Clapp & Jones, of Hudson, N. Y., and are now known as the "American Fire-Engine Co."

RICHARD HARRELL — 1869.

The first three Steam Fire-Engines constructed by Richard Harrell of Paterson, N. J., the first of which he built in 1869, were made from designs of Mr. John Nichols, master workman in the Grant Locomotive Works of that city. Mr. Nichols only built

PASSAIC ENGINE NO. I, PATERSON, N. J.
Built by Richard Harrell.

one, which was in 1867, and it was sold in the following year to the city of Paterson, N. J., Mr. Harrell at that time being a stockholder.

This machine was straight frame and very simple in construction, having two double acting pumps placed horizontally with frame which measured $4\frac{1}{4}$ inches in diameter with 9 inch stroke of piston — steam cylinders $6\frac{1}{2}$ inches in diameter, 9 inch stroke, worked with crank motion. The boiler was an upright tubular, 34 inches in diameter, and contained 262 $1\frac{1}{4}$ inch copper smoke flues. The weight of this machine when loaded and ready for service was 5,600 lbs. Mr. Harrell only built three of this same style. In 1871, the entire plant was destroyed by fire, at which time two machines, partly finished, were saved in a damaged condition and afterwards completed at the shops of Joseph Nussey & Co.

In the meantime, Mr. Harrell designed a somewhat different style of engine in four sizes; all of which were horizontal, and, with one exception, all were double. These machines were built at the shops of the Paterson Engine Works, of which Mr. Harrell was manager, and were models of beauty, especially one that was built for the Passaic Engine Co., No. 1, of Paterson, which in style and finish was elegant in the extreme. It was owned by the company, who took great pride and pleasure in visiting fire companies of other cities and placing their beautiful engine on exhibition; even taking it as far as Boston on one occasion, where it was greatly admired by all. This machine was double and of the horizontal pattern with straight frame of polished steel hung on half elliptic springs. All other parts were encased in bright finish of silver plate, brass, copper and princess metal, with fancy side lights and highly ornamented. The suction hose was carried squirrel tail fashion, connected at the forward part of the engine to the pumps. The wheels, which were of wood, showed the painter to be an artist.

The third-class engines of this style, of which five were built, had pumps 5 inches in diameter, $7\frac{1}{2}$ inch stroke, steam cylinders 8 inches in diameter, $7\frac{1}{2}$ inch stroke, with crank motion. The boilers were $31\frac{1}{2}$ inches in diameter, and contained 265 $1\frac{1}{4}$ inch smoke flues. Total weight, including water and fuel, 5,000 lbs.

The fourth class, of which twelve were built, were of the same general style, only smaller, having pumps $3\frac{7}{8}$ inches in diameter with $6\frac{1}{2}$ inch steam cylinders. The boilers were 29 inches in diameter, containing 234 flues. This size weighed 4,000 lbs.

This firm went out of existence in 1874. In 1876, Mr. Joseph Nussey built one engine for the city of Paterson of the old original type, which is now occasionally used. This was the last engine built from these patterns.

JUCKET & FREEMAN — 1869.

Outside of the New England States, but little is seen or heard about the engines built by Jucket & Freeman, of Roxbury, Mass., which were equal, if not superior, to any steam fire-engine ever built in the Bay State. Their first steamer was built at their shops

NORTHERN LIBERTY, No. 8, BOSTON.
Built by Jucket & Freeman.

on Hampden Street, in 1869, was sold to the city of Boston and was known as " Northern Liberty," No. 8. This machine was what is termed a straight-frame with double vertical pumps and steam cylinders, and of the following dimensions: pumps, 4½ inches in diameter, 8 inch stroke; steam-cylinders, 7¼ inch diameter, 8 inch stroke. The pumps were double action, each having a valve shell, square in section, divided vertically by a horizontal partition. One face carried eight rubber suction valves, the opposite face

8 discharge valves, $3\frac{1}{4}$ inches in diameter, of the "Poppet" pattern. The crank shaft was divided, and so coupled that either pump could be run separate if desired. The boiler was of the tubular pattern, with 199 $1\frac{1}{2}$ inch smoke tubes. A series of circulating tubes were placed in the fire-box, close to the leg, and connected with both crown-sheet and leg. All the iron work was polished. The boiler, steam-cylinders and feed water-tank were encased with a beautiful fluted jacket.

It was the pride of its engineer, Mr. Brown S. Flanders, and was, at one time, considered the handsomest and best engine in the city. The latter is well-proven, as she has outworn all the others that were in service when she was put in commission, and is still in active use and good for many years to come. This is the only one in the Boston Department that was at the great fire of Nov. 9, 1872, which has not been discarded.

The weight of this engine is 8,500 lbs. While in business, this firm built five engines, four double and one light single engine. In 1871, the business was discontinued owing to mismanagement on the part of Mr. Jucket, who was an expert mechanic, but otherwise incompetent. Mr. Francis Freeman became connected with Engine 13 of the Boston Department, and was for sixteen years foreman of that company, which was running the second steamer which he built while in business, and which also proved to be an excellent machine, having been put in service in the spring of 1870, and doing continuous duty until 1895, when it was discarded on account of the breaking of some of its castings which could not be duplicated on account of the patterns being destroyed. He retired from the service in 1887.

Mr. Jucket went to Providence, R. I., and secured a position in the fire department of that city as stoker, but died soon after.

The patterns of these engines were sold to the Union Machine Co., of Fitchburg, Mass., where several more of them were manufactured, but they shortly afterwards gave up the business. Later on, two or three more were built at the Allen Supply Co.'s works at Providence, R. I.

JOHN L. KNOWLTON — 1872.

John L. Knowlton built several Steam Fire-Engines at Sharon Hill, Delaware Co., Pa., five of which were sold to the Philadelphia Fire Department. These machines were all single pump and steam cylinder, and of the vertical pattern, with link motion. The pumps were 5 and $5\frac{1}{4}$ inches in diameter, with 11 and 12 inch stroke of piston, and weighed about 7,500 lbs. as drawn to fires. The frames were built both straight and crane neck. The boiler was of the ordinary tubular style. In 1885, Campbell & Rickards of Philadelphia built at their shops five engines for the Philadelphia Department, under

BUILT BY JOHN L. KNOWLTON.

the supervision of H. Johnson, foreman of the Fire Department Repairs, who patterned almost entirely from Knowlton's designs; all being single engines with 5 inch pump, 10 inch steam cylinder and 10 inch stroke; the weight being about 7,200 lbs. without fuel or water. Two double pump engines were afterwards built, having the same size pump and steam cylinder as the single engines. They weighed 10,000 lbs. One of them was afterwards altered over by Mr. George Rickards. The pump measured $6\frac{1}{2}$ inches in diameter — steam cylinder $11\frac{1}{2}$ inches in diameter, 10 inch stroke; weight 8,000 lbs. The frame was very high and slightly crooked at the forward end to allow the wheels to turn under. The boiler was of the "La France" pattern.

LA FRANCE MANUFACTURING CO. — 1875.

The La France Fire Engine Co., of Elmira, N. Y., taking into consideration that they are the youngest of successful firms now doing business, and have sold during their short career over 350 machines, goes to show that their engines are well up to the standard. This firm first commenced building steam fire-engines in 1875. They were of

LATEST IMPROVED DOUBLE ENGINE.

the rotary pattern and claimed to be the most perfect rotary pump then in use. The engine consisted of a pair of gears, having but few and very strong teeth, interlocking with each other and running together within a steam-tight case, making ten exhausts to one revolution of the shaft. The pumps were a duplicate of the steam-cylinders in form. The special improvement consisted in side packing plates in the steam-cylinders for taking up the differential expansion in the gears and case at the different temperatures of steam, and in adjustable packing plates in the pump-case, following up the wear of the

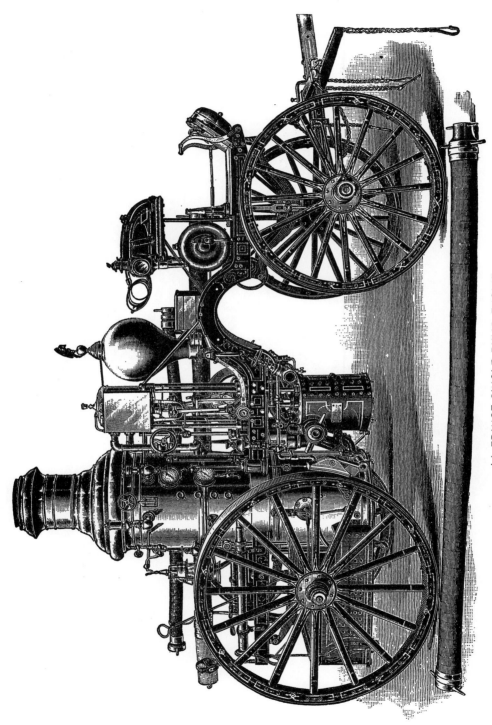

LA FRANCE SINGLE PUMP ENGINE.

LA FRANCE ROTARY ENGINE

teeth. The packing plates in the engine prevented all leakage of steam, and yielded to the expansion of the gears without producing undue friction. The packing plates in the pumps were adjusted without opening them or stopping the engine. The boiler had a complete and rapid circulation, and by the arrangement of its flues, a larger heating surface was obtained within a given diameter than most other boilers, and steam could be raised in between four and five minutes. These engines worked with very little friction, and the steadiness can well be imagined when a glass full of water could be placed upon a wheel and the machine worked at its utmost capacity without a drop of water being spilt from the tumbler.

These engines were built in five sizes and were capable of discharging from 350 to 750 gallons of water per minute. Good results were obtained from these engines where

LA FRANCE PUMP.

LA FRANCE PUMP, SIDE VIEW.

practical men had them in charge who were not prejudiced. But, as there were vast opinions as to the superiority between the rotary and piston steam fire-engine, this firm, with an eye to business, resolved to be prepared to furnish both, and in 1885 announced that they were ready to build piston engines in seven sizes. These machines were all of the vertical pattern. The four largest weighed from 7,500 to 4,800 lbs., and were double; the three smallest were single, weighing from 4,500 to 4,000 lbs., all being crane-neck style of frame. The boiler is of an improved pattern. The crown-sheet is placed three inches below the top of the fire-box sheet, from which are suspended a series of nest or water-tubes, comprising nine $1\frac{1}{4}$ inch tubes, connected by right and left hand threads to malleable iron headers which connect with leg of boiler at the bottom, while the top is connected through the crown-sheet by a pipe which protrudes three inches above the crown-sheet, leaving at all times a quantity of water upon the same. The smoke-tubes are arranged to encircle the nest-headers, making a direct draught for the flame through the nests, and leading directly through the boiler to the stack above, passing near the top of the boiler to the diaphragm sheet. The opening in this sheet is slightly larger than the smoke-flue, leaving an ample space through which the steam passes to the space above, that serves as a steam drain from whence the steam pipe carries it to the engine. A little above the crown-sheet, a ring shaped cross section is attached to the inner surface of the boiler-shell, forming a receptacle for mud or other impurities in the water which is carried upward by the natural circulation of the water.

Mud plugs are provided for cleaning and washing this space. There are two force-pumps provided for feeding the boiler, easy of access and simple in construction, the water from which is fed into the boiler under the fire-box door, for the purpose of preventing the collection of scales or mud under the door ring. These boilers are also provided with dumping grates. The steam and water-cylinders are bolted to bed-plates fastened to the frame, and their only connection to the boiler is the short steam pipe and a brace. The piston-rods are connected by a yoke and are worked by a connecting rod fastened at the top by a crank motion, no link blocks being used.

The latest principal improvement made on their piston-engines is on their pumps which are not only novel in construction, but which possess, in an eminent degree, all the essential points of simplicity, ease of dismounting, lightness in weight, strength and large capacity. The shell, which is cylindrical in form, top and bottom heads, pump-cylinders and stuffing boxes being cast, as they are, in one piece, which avoids a possibility of a leakage at the heads, is another good point.

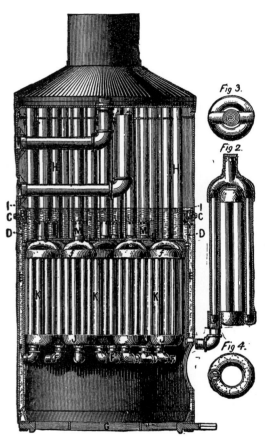

LA FRANCE NEST-TUBE BOILER.

An examination of the pump-valves or interior mechanism is but the work of a few minutes in unscrewing the lids which are arranged in the front of the pump, and when removed, expose all the valves grouped in the closest relation to each other. These engines are hung on platform springs forward, and half-elliptical behind, and are very beautifully finished in full nickel-plate, unless ordered otherwise. The largest and most powerful of these engines is what is termed their Extra First Size, the pumps of which measure $5\frac{3}{4}$ inches in diameter, with 9 inch stroke of piston; steam cylinders, $9\frac{3}{4}$ inches in diameter, 9 inch stroke; weight 8,200 lbs., without fuel or water. These machines are said to be capable of discharging 1,100 gallons of water per minute.

EATON & PRINCE—1875.

Eaton & Prince of Chicago, Ill., commenced building Steam Fire-Engines in 1875, and during the three years of their business in that line, constructed about twelve machines.

BUILT BY EATON & PRINCE.

These engines were built in but one size, weighed about 6,000 lbs., and were arranged to be drawn by horse or hand, and were intended to take the place of hand-engines in small cities and towns where cost was to be taken into consideration. They were what is termed a "Mongrel" engine, this being a cross between a piston and rotary motion. The boilers used were vertical and tubular, of the Amoskeag make. The steam cylinders were double, and bolted to the boiler in a vertical position with a slight cant, and were 6 inches in diameter with 6 inch stroke of piston.

(119)

Below the steam cylinders was a rotary pump 7 inches in diameter, with two solid balance wheels, one on either side, which were fastened to a shaft that passed through the pump. From a crank-pin on the balance wheels were connecting rods which were fastened to the sliding blocks of the steam pistons, which gave the pump its movement. The air chambers were small, of cylindrical shape and placed directly over the pump, from which were two outlets. The inlet was at the bottom of the pump, with a goose-neck connection, to which the suction hose was attached at all times. The frame was of the crane neck style.

The finish of these engines was very plain, which enabled the builders to sell them at the remarkably low price of $1,800.

KNOWLES STEAM PUMP WORKS — 1875.

Several portable Steam Fire-Engines have been constructed by this firm at their Works at Warren, Mass. The first style built was equipped with an ordinary tubular boiler with any sized pump as the purchaser might desire; the No. 6 pump being generally ordered, which was of the following dimensions: pump 5 inches in diameter,

KNOWLES STEAM ENGINE.
Built by the Knowles Steam Pump Works.

steam cylinder 7½ inches in diameter, with 10 inch stroke, a boiler of 8 horse power being used with this size of pump. The weight was about 4,700 lbs., the price being $800, when finished in the plainest possible manner.

About 1880, another style of engine was constructed by them, being furnished with what is known as the "Shapley Patent Return Tubular Boiler"; the accompanying cut of which will give the reader a correct idea. This boiler, as shown, is in two sections; the lower section containing the greater part of the fire-box and all the tubes, both vertical and horizontal. The vertical tubes are situated between the fire-box and the outside shell of the boiler, having their lower ends terminate in the smoke chamber which nearly

surrounds the ash-pit, and which extends to the smoke-stack at the rear of the boiler. The upper section is principally a reservoir for steam. The fire-box extends a short distance into this upper section. The hot gases are conveyed through the short cross-tubes to the vertical tubes and thence to the smoke-chamber as shown by the arrows in the engraving. The tubes and crown-sheets, as will be seen, are removed as far as possible from the intense heat of the fire. All the heating surfaces are below the water line, hence no liability to burn out the boiler. This is a very important feature, and adds materially to the durability of the boiler. The combustion chamber being unusually large, perfect combustion ensues. Any kind of fuel can be used, which is a matter of great convenience in case of emergencies. The large reservoir for steam in this boiler overcomes the difficulty in most boilers of priming or making wet steam. Easy access to the tubes is obtained by means of the bonnet which surrounds the boiler outside, between the upper and lower sections. This bonnet is made in sections and can be easily

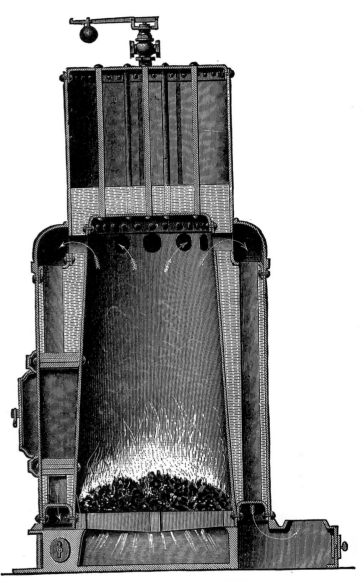

SHAPLEY PATENT BOILER.

removed, the tubes cleaned with flue brush and replaced. A six-horse-power boiler of this kind is generally used with pump and steam-cylinder of the following dimensions : pump, $5\frac{1}{2}$ inches in diameter, steam-cylinder, $5\frac{1}{2}$ inches in diameter, with 7 inch stroke of piston. The weight of these engines is about 4,000 lbs., and price $700. Several of these machines have been built for the Khedive of Egypt. They were designed expressly for the West Indian and South American trade for irrigating, draining and fire-service. A sectional view of the Knowles Pump, used on these engines, with explanation of parts, is given below.

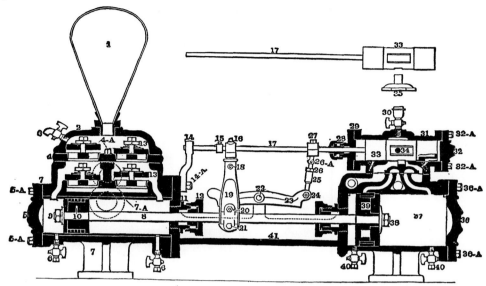

PARTS OF KNOWLES PUMP.

1. Air Chamber. 2. Water Cap. *2A. Water Cap Swing Bolt, complete, with Nut, Washer and Pin. 3. Air Cock. 4. Valve Plate or "False Seat." 4A. Valve Plate Bolt. 5. Water Cylinder Head. 5A. Water Cylinder Head Bolt. 6. Drip Cocks for Water Cylinder. 7. Water Cylinder or Working Barrel including Lining and Suction Valve Seats, but no other parts. 7A. Brass Lining for Water Cylinder or Working Barrel. 8. Piston Rod, complete with Nuts and Lock Nuts for both ends. 9. Piston Rod Nut and Lock Nut (Water End). 10. Water Piston (canvas packed), complete, embracing Head, Follower, Follower Bolts, Segments and Packing. 10A. Water Piston Head. 10B. Water Piston Follower. *10C. Water Piston Follower Bolt. 10D. Water Piston Packing, per lb. *10E. Water Piston Segments, per set. 11. Piston Rod Stuffing Box, complete (same on Steam End). 11A. Piston Rod Stuffing Box Seat. 11B. Piston Rod Stuffing Box Follower. 12. Piston Rod Stuffing Box Nut or Gland. 13. Pump Valve (specify the kind, as below). 13A. Rubber Valve, "Soft" for cold water. 13B. Rubber Valve, "Hard," for hot water. 13C. Rubber Valve Seat. 13D. Rubber Valve Stem. 13E. Rubber Valve Spring. *13F. Metal "Disk" Valve complete, with Seat, Spring and Nut. *13G. Hinge Valve, complete, with Seat. *13H. Ball Valve, complete, with Seat. *13I. Cage Valve, complete, with Seat, Spring and Nut. *13J. Cage Valve Drops, each. 14. Valve Rod Guide. 14A. Valve Rod Guide Bolt. 15. Valve Rod Collar, including Set-Screw and Gib. 15A. Valve Rod Collar Set-Screw. 15B. Valve Rod Collar Gib. 16. Tappet Arm Tip. 17. Valve Rod. 18. Tappet Tip Set-Screw. 19. Tappet Arm, complete, with Tip, Tip Set-Screw and Lower Bolt and Nut. 20. Rocker Roller. 20A. Rocker Roller Stud and Nut. 21. Tappet Arm Lower Bolt and Nut. 22. Rocker Bar Bolt and Nut. *22A. Rocker Bar Bolt Set-Screw. 23. Rocker Bar. 24. Rocker Connection Bolt and Nut. 25. Rocker Connection. 26. Rocker Connection Set Nut. 26A. Ball Joint and Nut. 27. Valve Rod Clamp, including Bolts and Gib. 27A. Valve Rod Clamp Bolts, each. 27B. Valve Rod Clamp Gib. 28. Valve Rod Stuffing Box Nut or Gland. 28A. Valve Rod Stuffing Box Follower. 29. Back Steam Chest Head which combines the Seat for Valve Rod Stuffing Box. 30. Lubricator. 31. Steam Chest, complete (includes Heads, with their Bolts; Chest Piston and its Guide Pin; Valve Rod and its Stuffing Box, complete; Valve Rod Clamp, Bolts and Gib; Valve Rod Collar Set-Screw and Gib; Tappet Arm Tip; Main Side Valve, Ball Joint and Nut). 31A. Steam Chest, without any parts. *31B. Steam Chest Holding Down Bolts, each. 32. Front Steam Chest Head. 32A. Front Steam Chest Head Bolts (same for back head). 33. Chest Piston. 34. Steam Chest Pin. 35. Main Slide Valve. 36. Steam Cylinder Head. 36A. Steam Cylinder Head Bolts. 37. Steam Cylinder, without any parts. 38. Piston Rod Nut and Lock Nut (Steam End). 39. Steam Piston, complete, embracing Head, Follower, Follower Bolts, Packing Rings, Studs and Springs. 39A. Steam Piston Head. 39B. Steam Piston Packing Ring. 39C. Steam Piston Follower. *39D. Steam Piston Follower Bolts, each. *39E. Steam Piston Packing Studs, per set. *39F. Steam Piston Packing Springs. 40. Steam Cylinder Cocks. †41. Centre Piece (casting between Steam and Water Cylinders).

* Not shown in cut.
† Pumps up to No. 3 have both Steam and Water Cylinders made in one casting; No. 3, No. 4 and No. 4½ Pumps, have Steam Cylinder and centre piece in one casting. In larger size Pumps, the centre piece is a separate casting from both Steam or Water Cylinders.

HILL & MOORLEN — 1879.

The Steam Fire-Engines built by Messrs. Hiram H. Hill and Frank Moorlen, of Augusta, Me., were of an entirely new invention, and were secured by letters patent in the United States and Canada, in 1878. Only two of these machines were constructed; the first, of which the cut is an accurate respresentation, was built in 1879, and sold to the city of Augusta, Me., and there known as Atlantic, No. 2. The claim of the

BUILT BY FRANK MOORLEN & CO., AUGUSTA, MAINE.

builders of these engines, was the reduction of friction to a minimum. This machine, as will be seen by the engraving, had a very peculiar shaped frame, which was bolted high up on the boiler, and slightly curved, which allowed the front wheels to turn under. Another noticeable feature, which differed entirely from that of any other make, was the manner of imparting motion to the fly-wheel shaft. The steam-cylinders, which were double, measured $9\frac{1}{2}$ inches in diameter, with 12 inch stroke, and were placed directly over a pair of double acting pumps, which measured $4\frac{1}{2}$

inches in diameter, with 12 inch stroke. Pistons were attached to the opposite end of a common piston rod, to the centre of which, between the pump and steam-cylinder, was attached a short crosshead, whose ends carried short connecting rods or links, which were riveted to the end of a lever or half walking-beam, in the end of which there was a guide-pole, through which the piston rod passed. This lever was pivoted at the other end to the frame of the engine, and between the piston rod and the middle of the lever was pivoted the main connecting rod, the lower end of which connected with the crank on the main or fly-wheel shaft. The feed pumps were also worked from this lever. All the motions and movements were on journals in composition boxes, which required no more oil than any ordinary machinery journals. The weight of this engine, when loaded for duty, was 6,740 lbs., and it cost $3,500. The boiler was of the common tubular style. This machine was used for several years in the Augusta Fire Department, but was finally disposed of, as it was no longer required on account of a high water service. It was purchased by the town of Livermore Falls, Me., where it is still used. The second and last engine built by this firm was of a smaller size, and was sold to Hallowell, Me.

MANSFIELD MACHINE WORKS — 1883.

On June 14, 1881, patents for a Steam Fire-Engine were granted the Mansfield Machine Works, of Mansfield, Ohio, which company had for the last thirty years an extensive experience in the construction of steam and pumping machinery. Their first

ROTARY ENGINE.
Built by the Mansfield Machine Works.

engine was completed in 1883, and was finished very plainly and void of all ornamentation, their effort being to procure an engine suitable to take the place of hand-engines in small towns and villages, at a moderate cost.

These machines were built in two sizes, and were of the following dimensions: first size, height over all, 8 feet 9 inches; width over all, 5 feet 8 inches; length over all (with tongue), 21 feet 8 inches; length over all (without tongue), 12 feet 9 inches;

capacity, 350 gallons per minute ; price, $2,000 : second size, height over all, 8 feet 3 inches ; width over all, 5 feet 8 inches ; length over all (with tongue), 20 feet 3 inches ; length over all (without tongue), 12 feet 3 inches ; capacity, 350 gallons per minute ; price, $1,500.   The weight of these engines was about 5,000 lbs., without water or fuel.   The difference in price was mostly owing to the first size having a more expensive finish.

The steam-cylinders on these engines were double and of the oscillating pattern, 4½ inches in diameter, 8 inch stroke, which worked on quarter centre cranks, and were simple and few in parts, having only one steam chest and no eccentrics, crossheads or slides.   The crank shaft, piston rods and connections were made from steel, solid gun metal crank shaft boxes, ground joints, case hardened bolts and studs, and self-setting steam piston packing.   The pumps were of the rotary pattern, similar to the " Holly," and were connected directly to the main engine shaft which was of large size, made from the best of steel and run in long gun metal boxes.   The gearing was also of steel, cut from the solid.   The boiler was made from the best selected C. H. No. 1 Boiler Plate, with Otis steel fire box.   The straight seams were all double riveted, and all heads doubly braced and stayed.   The outside diameter was 36 inches; height, 5 feet 6 inches; inside diameter of fire box, 32 inches; height inside, 20 inches, and it had 250 full weight, lap welded, submerged boiler tubes, 20 inches long.   This boiler was guaranteed to raise steam from cold water in from four to eight minutes.   Either dumping or standing grates were furnished, as desired.   All trimmings, such as gauges, whistle and pop valve, were made from the best of steam metal.   The boiler was supplied with water by a patent independent steam pump, which was entirely independent of the main engine, and could be worked by hand if desired.   The boiler could also be fed from the main pump.   The boiler was hung forward of the rear axle on easy and substantial springs. The frame was made of the best charcoal hammered iron, being well braced and stayed. The wheels were hand made, with sawed felloes and hand-shaved spokes made from choice selected timber with iron hubs.   The diameter of hind wheels was 60 inches, front wheels 40 inches.

These engines were furnished complete with suction-hose, lamps, wrenches and firing tools, and were made to be drawn by horses or hand as desired.   The following is a report of a trial of one of these machines costing $1,500.

"THE PAULDING CHIEFTAIN."

From the Paulding, Ohio, *Democrat*, January 31, 1884 :—

The new Fire-Engine recently ordered from the Mansfield, Ohio, Machine Works by our "city dads," was given a fair test trial on the streets Wednesday afternoon of last week, and its work proved satisfactory to our citizens far beyond expectation.   The Engine is a New Model, Rotary Pump Steamer, designed to take the place of the largest hand engines in all places and under all circumstances.   The excellent work it did on trial here is evidence that it more than fills the bill for that purpose and shows that the builders have displayed great skill in its make up and used the best material in its manufacture. Two hose attachments of 400 feet were made and two streams thrown 200 feet through $\frac{5}{8}$ inch nozzles. One attachment was made with 200 feet, and a stream was thrown 240 feet with a $\frac{3}{4}$ inch nozzle. Then 700 feet of hose was put on and through a $\frac{3}{4}$ inch nozzle a stream was forced 210 feet. Steam was made in the boiler in six minutes, from cold water, and in nine minutes water could have been thrown. The engine is not heavy, and can be easily handled by a small force of men on ordinarily

DOUBLE PISTON ENGINE.
Built by the Mansfield Machine Works.

good roads. While in action, it worked nicely in all its parts; all the competent judges here pronouncing it complete. Paulding people feel no little pride in the new investment, and we believe that the Mansfield Machine Works,—of which Mr. N. Abbott is superintendent,—run no risk in giving their engines a strong guarantee. The comparatively low price at which these engines are furnished makes it possible for Paulding to procure a steamer at a time when it would not seem profitable to invest such an amount as would be necessary to purchase one of the large, old style machines. At a meeting of the Village Council Monday evening, it was unanimously resolved to accept the Engine, and the contract was complete. It has been named the "Paulding Chieftain."

The latest production from this firm is a double vertical engine, with piston pumps, link motion, highly finished and well adapted for city use. They are mounted on crane-neck frame with platform springs forward and half-elliptical behind. The pumps measure 4½ inches in diameter with 8 inch stroke of piston, steam-cylinder 7 inches in diameter, 8 inch stroke. The price of this machine is $3,500, and it is considered an A No. 1 machine. About 50 engines have been sold by this company, who are still in the business, and who claim that their machines have given good satisfaction.

GEORGE F. BLAKE — 1885.

The pumps built by the George F. Blake Manufacturing Co., of Boston, Mass., have a world-wide reputation.   In 1885, a portable boiler and pump engine designed expressly for the West Indian, South American and Southern trade, and especially adapted for irrigating, drainage and fire service, and for general use about plantations, public grounds, etc., etc., was constructed for the United States Government, to be stationed at Fort Warren, Boston Harbor.   This engine was finished in the plainest possible manner, void of all ornamentation, such as dome, boiler-jacket, etc.   The frame was straight and

BUILT BY THE BLAKE MANUFACTURING CO.

of wrought iron, upon which was placed, in a horizontal position, a single double-acting No. 7 Blake Pump, measuring 6 inches in diameter, with 12 inch stroke ; steam-cylinder, 10 inches in diameter, 12 inch stroke.   Suspended from this frame was a large feed-water tank to supply the boiler with fresh water, a No. 00 pump being used for that purpose.   The boiler was of the ordinary tubular style.   This machine was fitted to throw two streams and was capable of doing good work.   The price paid for it was $1,100.   Although these engines never met with approval in the fire-service of cities and towns, they have admirably fulfilled the purpose for which they were expressly designed.

(130)

THOMAS MANNING, JR., & CO. — 1886.

The engines built by Thomas Manning, Jr., & Co., of Cleveland, Ohio, are fast becoming very popular, and bid fair to become one of the leading Steam Fire-Engines of the day. Although young in the business of building, they have repaired and rebuilt engines for a great many years, which has given them the knowledge as to what is required to constitute a first-class machine.

Their first engine was constructed in 1886, and like all their succeeding engines, was vertical with double steam cylinder and double acting pumps, Mr. Thomas Manning, Jr., being the designer of the motion work and Mr. Charles R. Moore the patentee of the boiler. These engines are being built at the present time in four sizes, but they are prepared to furnish them in any size to suit the demand.

Their largest or first size machine has steam-cylinders 8½ inches in diameter, 9-inch stroke. Pumps 5 inches in diameter, 9-inch stroke. Weight 6,650 lbs., without fuel or water. Price $4,250. The steam-cylinders of the second-class measure 8¼ inches in diameter, 8-inch stroke of piston. Pumps 4¾ inches in diameter, 8-inch stroke. Weight about 6,650 lbs. Price $3,800. The third-class has steam-cylinders 7⅜ inches in diameter, 8-inch stroke. Pumps 4¼ inches in diameter, 8-inch stroke. Weight 5,820 lbs. Price $3,450. The fourth, or smallest size, has steam-cylinders 6¾ inches in diameter, 8-inch stroke. Pumps 4 inches in diameter, 8-inch stroke. Weight 5,400 lbs. Price $3,200.

The pumps of these engines are very similar to the Amoskeag, the valves being top and bottom, excepting that they have in each pump 10 inlet and 6 outlet valves instead of 8 inlet and 8 outlet. The piston rods receive their motion by what is termed a crank and connecting rod movement, there being no link blocks used. The steam end is the ordinary D slide valve. The boiler is pronounced by experts to be one of the best steam makers in the country, size and weight being considered. It is entirely new in fire-engine construction and is of the following description. It is a copper water tube boiler and consists of two shells, with a one-inch water space below at the leg, and a 5-inch steam space at the top between the two shells. In the lower part of this boiler is hung a section with composition heads and copper tubes, which is connected with nipples at the leg, and to the upper part with elbows into the steam and water space, this being the steam generating section. In the upper part of the inner shell is hung the upper section, also of copper tubes and composition heads. At the bottom of this section, the feed water enters and passes through the entire section of tubes to the top and then down between the two shells through copper pipes, and is discharged (at the steaming point) below the normal water line, the steam rising to the steam space, and the water flowing down the leg of boiler, and circulating through the generating section.   A feature which will be readily appreciated by engineers is the absence of heads from this boiler, and all the inside being of copper, making them practically indestructible, which should outlast the shells, while in other boilers the shell usually outlasts two or three sets of tubes and heads.   A 32-inch boiler of this description carries 53 gallons of water at a safe working point.

BUILT BY THOMAS MANNING, JR., & CO.

At a delivery trial of one of these engines at Erie, Pa., the pressure gauge hand began to move in 2½ minutes after the torch was applied to the furnace, and forty pounds of steam was registered in five minutes.

The following is an account of a test of one of their Fourth-Class Engines.

"MANNING'S ENGINE."

"The successful test of the new Fire Engine was the subject at Fire Headquarters, Friday, and Thomas Manning was congratulated by all the officials.   Particular interest attached to the trial for the reason that the new engine was equipped with an entirely new type of sectional water tube boiler. Its peculiar merits, as explained by Mr. Manning, are safety, quick steaming, durability and light weight. Then its accessibility is such that the entire 'insides' can be removed in less than two hours. The boiler is but 28 inches in diameter and 59 inches high, furnishing ample steam for two 6¾-inch steam-cylinders, 8-inch stroke, and pumps 4 inches in diameter, 8-inch stroke. As a water thrower the engine is a giant, and considered an acquisition to the fire department.

" Six tests were made. The results of the different tests are as follows :

	Steam lbs. Pressure.	Water lbs.	Size of Nozzle.	Dis. Thrown.
First test	120	165	1⅛ in.	246 ft.
Second test	120	145	1¼ in.	238 ft.
Third test	110	135	1⅜ in.	226 ft.
Fourth test	125	154	1¼ in.	250 ft.
Fifth test	140	190	1⅜ in.	248 ft.
Sixth test	120	150	2 in.	205 ft.

" The first three tests were made with two 50-foot lines siamized into one 50-foot line. The others were made with lines each 200 feet long, smooth bore nozzles being used. On the whole, the tests were highly satisfactory to the officials, and the wonderful performance of the little engine was the subject of many highly complimentary remarks from practical firemen and mechanical experts. The engine is handsome in appearance, very compactly built. Director Hyman, Chiefs Dickinson and Rebbeck, ex-Chief Shay, of Chicago, Chief Manderbauh, and F. F. Loomis, of Akron, were present."

Ten of these engines are in service in the Cleveland Fire Department at the present time and all are reported as giving good satisfaction.

WATEROUS ENGINE WORKS CO. — 1888.

This firm, as near as can be ascertained, commenced the building of Steam Fire-Engines at St. Paul, Minn., in 1888. Whether they are still building, or the success they met with while in the business, cannot be ascertained, as several letters written to them failed of a reply. The cut represents one of their No. 1 engines, which was designed specially for towns and villages having volunteer fire companies, and was known as the "Village Steam Fire-Engine." The price for this engine was $2,000; dimensions as follows; Capacity 300 gallons per minute. Weight 2,500 lbs. Extreme height 6 feet

WATEROUS ENGINE.

8 inches. Extreme length, with pole, 18 feet 6 inches; without pole, 9 feet 6 inches. Tread of wheels 4 feet. The pumps were of the " Duplex Piston " pattern, with a patent compound valve motion of a special design, by which device, all cranks and eccentrics were omitted. The boiler (on which they held letters patent) was also of a new design, having no circulating pipes, nest-tubes, drop-tubes or coil-pipes. Claim was made that it could not be exploded except designedly or through the very grossest carelessness on the part of the man running it.

The following is from the Perry, Iowa, *Advertiser* of Oct. 6, 1888 : —

" Last Thursday in the presence of the Mayor and Council, the new Steam Fire-Engine, purchased from the Waterous Engine Works Co., of St. Paul, Minn., was officially tested according to the contract the city had made. By order of Frederick Knell, Chief of the Fire Department, the engine was placed at the tank at the Triangle. The first test was the time of getting up steam from cold water. Alderman Dr. Trout, who kept the time, gave the record as follows : first sign of steam 1¾ minutes, 5 lbs. in 2 minutes, 10 lbs. in 3 minutes, 20 lbs. in 4 minutes, 40 in 6¼ minutes. In 6¾ minutes from time of lighting fire, a stream was thrown over the new Wimmer Building. This test more than fulfilled the terms of the contract as to quick steaming, which was to raise steam and throw water in from 8 to 12 minutes.

" The next test was through two lines of hose of 300 feet each, using ¾-inch nozzles. These were really two beautiful streams and were forced fully 40 feet higher than the highest building in the city.

" Test No. 3 was distance of throwing water through 500 feet of hose using 1-inch nozzle, a stream being thrown horizontally over 150 feet.

" For the fourth test, Chief Knell ordered 1,000 feet of hose to be laid and the engine turned over to the hands of Alderman J. Lessell, who apparently handled it as easily and successfully as did the delivering engineer, and with the exception of but one stop, occasioned by a bursting section of hose, kept a powerful stream playing for three-quarters of an hour.

" The Council and Chief Knell being satisfied that the Company had fulfilled the terms of the contract, no further trial was thought necessary. The engine, which is really a little beauty, is what the makers term their No. 1 size, being the smallest they make. Chief Knell and his men are proud of the new acquisition to their department and, when occasion requires, will no doubt give a good account of themselves. The engine has been accepted and settled for, and is now placed in service."

AMERICAN FIRE-ENGINE CO. — 1891.

The American Fire-Engine Co., of Seneca Falls, N. Y., and Cincinnati, Ohio, was incorporated under the laws of New York State on December 12, 1891, with a capital of $600,000, and is, at the present time, the most extensive corporation in the manufacture of Engines and Fire Department Supplies in the world. This company was formed by the consolidation of the following well known firms in the manufacture of Steam Fire Engines : Silsby Manufacturing Co., of Seneca Falls, N. Y., Ahrens Manufacturing Co., of Cincinnati, Ohio, Clapp & Jones Manufacturing Co., of Hudson, N. Y., and the Button Fire-Engine Co., of Waterford, N. Y., including real estate, machinery, tools, patterns, patents, and good will, with the following officers and managers : —

Hiram H. Nieman, President ; Du Bois Collier, Vice-President ; Charles T. Silsby, Treasurer ; William S. Silsby, Secretary ; Chris Ahrens, Mechanical Engineer ; Horace Silsby, G. F. Hawekotte, Du Bois Collier, George E. Holroyd, Managers.

The engines built by these companies during the past 35 years are too well known to need more than a passing mention, as they have all been referred to in other parts of this history. Their manufactories are now conducted under one management, with the mechanical experience of the several companies consolidated.

These well known types of engines are not only built in a more improved manner, but, with the combined mechanical skill now obtained, and having at their disposal all the special features of these engines, protected by patents heretofore controlled by the respective companies, they are enabled to satisfy the wishes of any purchaser by combining, in any one machine, such points of excellence and details of construction as may be desired. Since the consolidation of these four firms into one, a new piece of apparatus has been constructed and called the " Columbian Engine." This machine has been designed for service in the suburban fire stations of large cities, but is equally well adapted for use in smaller towns, combining, as it does, two distinct pieces of fire apparatus in one. The engine is built with double cylinders and pumps, placed vertical and of the Ahrens type. From the engine, extending to the extreme forward part, is a large and handsomely finished box, capable of carrying from 600 to 1000 feet of rubber lined cotton fire-hose and supplied with suitable rollers for running out the same. When the hose-box is closed, it may be used as a seat for the firemen, and as many as ten men can ride on the engine, if desired. The boilers of these engines are furnished according to the wishes of the purchasers, with choice of selection of either of the patterns which they manufacture ; the latest of which, is of a submerged flue style of improved construction. This boiler is made of the best homogeneous steel and strongly stayed. The flues are

COLUMBIAN ENGINE.

NEW "AMERICAN" ENGINE.

made of seamless copper and are so arranged that any single tube can be taken out without removing the boiler-head.   The flues are screwed into the upper head and rolled into the lower sheet, being entirely submerged at all times, thus preventing unequal expansion.   This machine is hung on platform springs in front and half elliptical springs in the

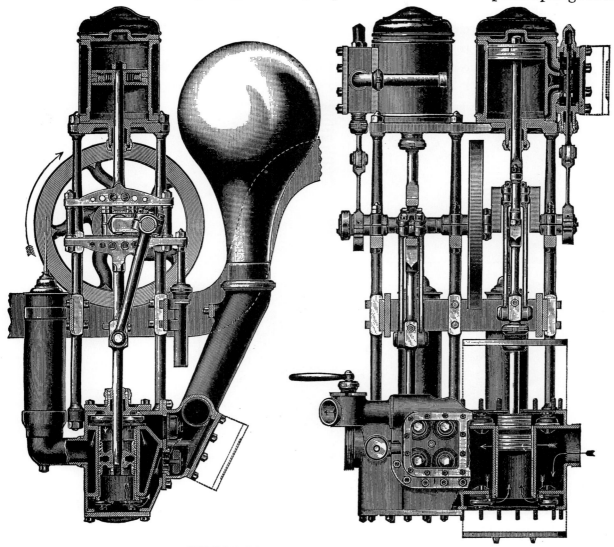

SECTION OF " NEW AMERICAN " ENGINE.

rear.   Combining, as it does, two distinct pieces of apparatus in one, it possesses advantages that will at once commend it to those engaged in the fire-service.   Being built light, it is easily handled on ordinary country roads, and is fitted to be drawn by horse or hand as preferred, and it is provided with every convenience that experience could suggest.

The " New American " engine built by this company is meeting with great approval and is built in six sizes, ranging in capacity from 400 to 1,300 gallons per minute, and is equipped with the submerged flue boiler. The pump is of an entirely new design, is an invention of their own and was first brought out by them in 1894. The claim they make is that it combines both the practical and theoretical requirements essential to a simple, reliable and efficient fire pump. These pumps, which are double acting, are united in a gun metal casing which forms a single body for both and permits them to be placed much closer as to centres than could otherwise be done. This method also obviates the usual weakness in construction attending a connection between separate pumps

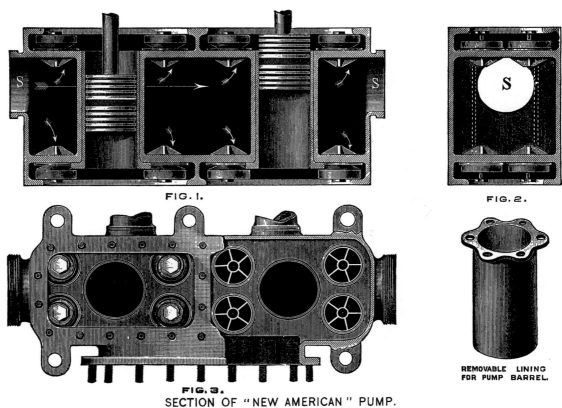

FIG. I.

FIG. 2.

REMOVABLE LINING
FOR PUMP BARREL.

FIG. 3.
SECTION OF "NEW AMERICAN" PUMP.

and provides an ample suction chamber which is common in both. It will be seen by reference to the cuts that any of the valves can be easily and quickly examined, and, if necessary, replaced by simply removing the caps and heads. The pump barrels are provided with removable linings which can readily be replaced with new ones in case the same should become worn after years of service. These, as well as the valve seats, are made from gun metal, no cast iron or other material subject to corrosion by water being used in any part of these pumps. The steam cylinders used in construction with this pump are of the ordinary slide valve type with which most mechanics are familiar and are thus easily repaired when necessary. They possess the sole right for use on Steam Fire-Engines of the Corliss patent ring packing. The cylinders and pumps are detached from the boiler and are separated therefrom sufficiently to allow every facility for getting at each and every part. All connections, both steam and water, are made outside of the boiler. The latest production of this firm is what is known as the special " American " export engine which is of special design and made expressly for export. It combines in its construction all the latest improvements. The fourth size capacity is 500 gallons per minute, weight 4,800 lbs., is 5 feet 9 inches in width, 8 feet 9 inches in height, and has a length, with pole, of 23 feet. It is equipped with the " New American " pump which is of the double acting type and their latest style of submerged flue boiler. The smaller sizes of this engine are fitted to be drawn by men as well as horses if desired. These engines are hung on a patent equalizing platform spring-rigging in front and on half elliptical springs in the rear. No matter what may be the position of the front wheels, the machine will always stand level and the strain on the wheels will be alike on both sides. The fixtures are all polished and nickel plated, and the frame, running gear and feed pan are handsomely painted. Each engine is supplied with suction hose, lanterns, gauges, tools, play pipes, nozzles and all other appointments, appurtenances and fixtures required for service. These engines for export are accompanied with full directions for setting up and operating them.

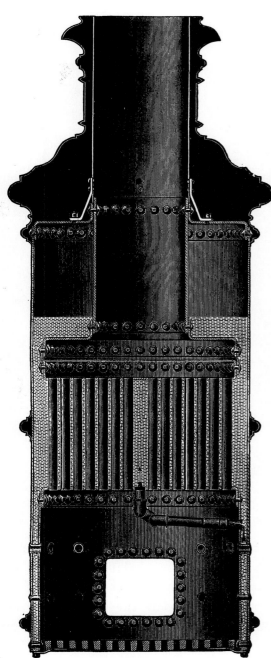

SUBMERGED FLUE BOILER.

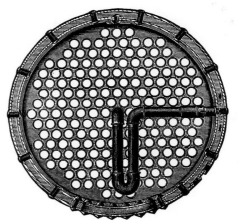

BOTTOM SECTION.

JAMES SMITH.

James Smith, the much noted Hand-Engine Builder, of New York City, commenced the manufacture of Steam Fire-Engines about the time of the Civil War. His engines were all of the horizontal pattern, with one single "double-acting" pump and steam-cylinder, straight frame with vertical tubular boiler, and were built to be drawn by horse or hand. The steam-cylinder was placed horizontally on the frame about one foot from the boiler

CONTINENTAL ENGINE NO. 9, BROOKLYN, N. Y.
Built by James Smith.

and the pump forward. A crosshead was attached to the piston-rod, to which were attached two connecting rods which connected with two solid iron balance-wheels at the rear of the steam cylinder. The inlet was at the bottom of the pump at the front of the engine; the outlets, two in number, were on the top of the pump at the base of the air-chamber, which was of the "Balloon" pattern. Quite a number of these engines were built and used in and about New York City with good results. The building of the Smith Engines was, however, of short duration, as they soon gave up the business.

JOSEPH BANKS.

Joseph Banks, of New York City, built seven steamers, the first of which was constructed about the year 1863. This firm, I am informed was at one time known as Clapp & Banks, and afterwards as Banks & Buckley. These engines were all of the horizontal pattern, with single pump and steam cylinder of M. R. Clapp's patent. In appearance, these engines very much resembled the "Smith."

A. B. TAYLOR, SON & CO.

A. B. Taylor, Son & Co., of New York City, also constructed three Steam Fire-Engines about the year 1865. In general appearance, they resembled both the "Smith" and "Banks," with the exceptions of the motion being crank instead of connecting rod and crosshead, and the balance wheels, being spoked instead of solid, were placed between the pump and steam cylinder. These machines were all single and of the horizon-

UNDINE ENGINE NO. 52.
Built by A. B. Taylor, Son & Co.

tal pattern. The pumps, which were invented by Mr. Hayes, of "Aërial Ladder" fame, were quite novel in regard to their valves, which were known as "Plug Valves"; each pump having two large plugs which screwed into the side of the pump, and each plug having two valves attached to it, one for receiving and one for delivery. "Undine Engine, No. 52," of New York City, at one time used one of these engines, which is, at the present time, in service in a Southern town.

BUILT BY ALLERTON & STEVENS.

ALLERTON & STEVENS.

Allerton & Stevens of New Haven, Conn., built only one engine, about the year 1885. This machine was a double horizontal, and, as the engraving shows, was a beautiful engine. The reason of their discontinuing the business is not known.

BUILT BY THE ARLINGTON IRON WORKS.

THE ARLINGTON IRON WORKS.

The Arlington Iron Works of Waverly, Iowa, constructed several Steam Fire-Engines, commencing about 1885; but the extent of their business or whether they have given it up cannot be ascertained, as letters failed to bring any reply. The cut represents one of their double horizontal machines.

HASKELL & JONES, of Albany, N. Y., built one Steamer in 1866, which was sold to the "Albany Steel Co." of Troy, N. Y. This engine was of the horizontal pattern with one steam-cylinder about 9 inches in diameter and about the same stroke of piston. The pump was of the semi or half rotary style. The connecting rods from the balance-wheels were attached to levers which dropped down from the pump and had a rocking motion. The weight of this machine was about 5,000 lbs., and it is reported that it could pass a great quantity of water, but was inferior on distance.

E. B. SINTGENICH, of Rochester, N. Y., built only one engine, which was in the year 1872. This machine was of the vertical pattern with one steam-cylinder measuring $10\frac{3}{4}$ inches in diameter, with $9\frac{1}{2}$ inch stroke. The pumps were double acting and two in number, having cylinders $4\frac{1}{4}$ inches in diameter with $9\frac{1}{2}$ inch stroke of piston. Both pumps received their up and down stroke together, as the piston rods were attached to the crosshead to which the steam piston rod was connected.

WATTS G. CORY, of Amsterdam, N. Y., built but one Steam Fire-Engine about the year 1873. He died shortly afterwards. This machine was vertical with link motion. This steam-cylinder measured 7 inches in diameter, pump 5 inches in diameter with 10 inch stroke of piston, and weighed 5,000 lbs. This engine is still in service in a small town in the central part of New York State, and is highly spoken of.

KNOULSON & KELLY, of Troy, N. Y., built one small engine in 1875 for the Troy Water Works to use for pumping out the water mains, etc., also to be used, if necessary, for fires.

THE SHEPPARD IRON WORKS, of Buffalo, N. Y., built several engines which were horizontal and double, with link motion.

The engines reported to have been built by A. E. Heaton, of New York City, Cobett & Co., of Milwaukee, Wis., and Kimball, of San Francisco, Cal., have become lost history.

SUGGESTIONS TO ENGINEERS.

The following suggestions were at one time given to engineers running Amoskeag Engines. These same directions will apply to almost every Piston Engine.

I.

In laying your fuel in the fire-box, first lay plenty of shavings, then light, dry kindling wood, filling your furnace full, which in most cases will give you steam enough by the time you arrive at a fire to commence work, providing you light your fire when you leave the house, which, as a general rule, is advisable.

II.

If you use coal, be careful to keep a thin fire, and not clog it. Use the coal in as large lumps as possible, and do not break it up unnecessarily in the furnace. The best coal for this purpose is a clean cannel, in lumps, free from dirt and dust.

III.

Be careful not to let so much fire collect under your engine as to burn the wheels. When working for a long time at fires there is some danger of doing so.

IV.

The Amoskeag boiler is an upright, tubular boiler, with a submerged smoke-box and fire-box surrounded with water. When the engine is running, the water in the boiler should be carried so as to stand at the third gauge-cock, which is placed near the top of the tubes, and it should never be carried below the centre of the tubes, at which point the first gauge-cock is located.

V.

Avoid using an unnecessary amount of steam. The tendency is to use more than is required. From sixty to eighty pounds is as much as you will generally require to do good fire duty.

VI.

The engine has two suitable feed-pumps for supplying the boiler with water. One of these pumps should be worked nearly all the time, in order to keep the water in the boiler at the proper height, and to preserve an even pressure of steam.

VII.

If brackish water is used for supplying the boiler, or if the boiler becomes foul from long use without being blown off, it is likely to foam or prime. If foaming occurs while the engine is working at a fire, it may be prevented or diminished by opening the surface blow-off cock, which is located between the third and fourth gauge-cocks, and blowing off from the surface of the water the scum and oily matter which usually causes foaming. In this way, the difficulty can generally be prevented without any serious interruption in

(148)

the working of the engine. While doing this, the water in the boiler should be carried as high as the surface blow-off cock. After the engine is returned to the house, the water should be blown entirely out of the boiler through the blow-off cock near the bottom of the boiler, with a steam pressure of about twenty pounds, and the boiler refilled with fresh water. This process may be repeated until the boiler becomes clean.

VIII.

The pump upon the Amoskeag engine is a vertical double-acting pump, with the cylinder surrounded by a circular chamber, divided vertically outside the cylinder, so as to answer both for the suction and discharge chambers of the pump. It has a separate valve-plate at the top and bottom of the pump, carrying both the suction and discharge valves, the suction-valve on one side of the plate, and the discharge-valve upon the other. Each of these valve-plates can be reached by taking off the top and bottom of the pump, which is so constructed as to be readily removed. The discharge and suction parts of the water-chamber surrounding the cylinder are connected by a valve in the vertical partition, which is called a relief-valve.

IX.

With a single long line of hose, it may be necessary to open your relief-valve a little, but at all other times be particular to have it closed, except when you want to feed your boiler without forcing any water through the hose.

X.

In the smoke-pipe, directly over the upper flue-sheet, a valve is placed which is called the variable exhaust valve. By operating this valve, the size of the aperture for the escape of the steam from the steam-cylinder is increased or diminished, thus regulating the draft of the chimney and the heat of the fire. This valve should be closed when the engine is started, until a fair working pressure of steam is obtained, after which it may be opened.

XI.

Care should be taken to have the suction-hose and its connections air-tight.

XII.

Open your discharge-gate and cylinder drain-cock before starting your engine.

XIII.

Don't let the flues of your engine get filled up.

XIV.

Be particular to take your engine off the springs before you work it, and to place it on the springs again when done working.

XV.

With a long line of hose on, be particular to open your throttle gradually. If you open it too suddenly, you are liable to burst your hose.

XVI.

The pumps of the engine should be examined at least once in six months, to see that the valves and all the parts are in good condition. The pump-valves should have a lift of about three-eighths of an inch, and the suction-valve the same lift.

XVII.

The inside of the steam-cylinders and the steam-valves should be oiled or tallowed always after the engine has worked at a fire, and as often as it may be necessary to keep them well lubricated ; and all the parts of the engine, where liable to friction, should be kept well oiled. Be particular to use an abundance of oil on the "link-block," where there is more friction than in any other part.

XVIII.

The running-gear and every part of the engine liable to disarrangement or accident should be thoroughly examined every time after the engine has been out of the house, whether it has been worked at the fire or not.

XIX.

Whenever your engine is repaired, try to help do it yourself, as by so doing you get a familiarity with it that you can obtain in no other way.

NOTE. — These suggestions are made more particularly for the benefit of engineers who have not had much experience in running engines.